IT TOOK A HUMAN
Revised Edition

ELSA HOLMES

For Mark and all those he has touched

Contents

FOREWORD

Hi! My name's Elsa. I'm a dog.

That's right, a dog. How can a dog write a book you ask? Well, I did. Now I'm a Great Pyrenees and I have huge paws. When I sit up at the computer, one paw covers half the keyboard. When I have both paws up there, I can't even read the letters. So my master, owner, and best friend, Dan Holmes, actually typed the manuscript for me. But I was right there with him the whole time, lying on the floor in the computer room or on the cool tile floor just outside, as he read each section aloud to get my approval before continuing. I'd say, "Yeah, sounds good. Go on." Then he'd read it again, and again I'd say, "Yes, it's fine, proceed." Then he'd read it again, and again, and again, ad infinitum, until I'd scream, "YES, DUDE, you got it! *Please* go on." Then he'd finally go on. Mister Dan knows me better than I know myself, so I think, in the end, he's captured my thoughts exactly.

Now I should pause here and explain that I'm a southern girl. I live in Florida. Down South, we always refer to our elders by their first name, as a term of endearment, but always preface it with Mister or Miss, as a sign of respect. So from now on I'll refer to my owners as Mister Dan and his wife as Miss Bev, and likewise for all other of my elders.

So how did this book come to be written? You see, Mister Dan wrote his own book last year called *IT TOOK A DOG*, also available on Amazon. Shortly after it was published, Mister Dan and Miss Bev went up to Aldie, Virginia, a suburb of Washington D.C., to visit their oldest son Scott and his wife Lauren. They have two kids, Lila and Wyatt. Wyatt had just been born a few weeks earlier so this was their first chance to meet their new grandson. Since they were going to be up there over a week, I got to go along. Scott, a strikingly handsome young man, had just read his Dad's book and really liked it. One evening when I was lying on the living room floor, Scott told his Dad he ought to write a second book but this time from my, the dog's, perspective. I perked up and looked at Scott. This kid's not only handsome, he's brilliant! I thought this was a famous idea, but Mister Dan said, "No, I'm done with my writing career," and just shrugged it off. But that night after I climbed the stairs and settled into sleep in the loft bedroom right next to the bed where Mister Dan and Miss Bev slept, I could tell Mister Dan was not sleeping and tossed and turned all night. This is the same thing that happened when he wrote his first book, *IT TOOK A DOG*, by Dan Holmes, available on Amazon. He'd think all night about what he wanted to say then write it down the next day. So my hope was that what his wise son had told him stuck with him. Turned out it did.

Now you're probably wondering if it is absolutely necessary for you to read Mister Dan's first book, *IT TOOK A DOG*, by Dan Holmes, available on Amazon, before reading this one? The answer is no. My book stands on its own. But it would help, as I use all the same chapter headings, with the exception of "The Extra Chapter" (which I'll talk about later) and I tell most of the same stories as in Mister Dan's book, and add a few more, but from my, the dog's, perspective. So this is a story about me, a Great Pyrenees named Elsa, and how Mister Dan changed my life. I will detail how I went from an abandoned rescue dog at an animal refuge, to my being adopted and finding my forever home, and eventually becoming a therapy dog. I will also detail the work Mister Dan and I do every week as a therapy dog team and stories about how we've touched and, occasionally, changed countless lives in our two and a half years together as a therapy dog team. I'll start at the beginning, before I ever met Mister Dan.

So who should read my book? Well, at times, my language can get a bit "salty." Why? Think about it. Who are my ancestors? Wolves, right? Every dog's ancient ancestor is the wolf. And you should hear a wolf talk. Especially when they get into packs, a wolf can cuss like a drunken sailor! So it's in my DNA. But Mister Dan said "NO, absolutely NOT." This book must remain appropriate for middle-schoolers and above, or for parents who want to read it to their kids. He said we must keep it PG rated. So the few times I feel very strongly about something and want to say it my way, Mister Dan will use a series of numbers and symbols to represent the word I *would* have said. I think you'll figure it out.

If you're a dog-lover, you must read this book. If you are, you've probably read a gazillion dog books, so why another one? Because I believe this is so much more than just a good dog book. I promise you'll laugh (I hope you already have), cry, and hopefully learn something you didn't already know about us dogs and other humans. If you're a dog-hater, you also need to read this book. Why? Because we have an epidemic of dog-haters in this country, as the countless animal shelters can attest when they see the abuse and mistreatment of dogs entering their facilities every day. Maybe, if you give it a chance, you too could learn something and more readily accept the canine friends that dog-lovers love. If you're a Great Pyrenees owner, or you know of someone who's owned a Great Pyrenees, like parents, a son or daughter, or just good friends, I hope I've already hooked you by my picture on the cover. The Great Pyrenees is the greatest dog breed on the planet. You'll want to read on as I'll explain why. And if I've totally ticked off all the Golden Retriever owners out there, hang with me. The Golden Retriever is the most popular dog breed in America, possibly in the whole world. And as a rescue dog, we're not totally sure I'm a pure-bred Great Pyrenees. I have a soft face like a Golden, so there may be some Golden Retriever in me. So take heart. I love my Golden friends too. If you're a human male, even though you don't show your emotions as much as your human female counterparts, I think you, too, can find some humor and much-needed tenderness in this book. If you're a human female, need I say more? Read on, and get your husband or boyfriend to read also.

So, I think that about covers it. If you don't fit into any of the above categories, then you aren't a member of the human race and you can crawl back into your cave and I won't bother you again. Otherwise, read on. But most of all, enjoy!

The First Chapter

I was cold. Even in northwest Florida, it gets cold at night in the wintertime. I was hungry. Oh, was I hungry. I was eating grass, weeds, leaves off of trees, branches, berries, even other dog's poop if I could find any. Disgusting, I know, but I've seen humans eat things just as disgusting. But most of all, I was lost – hopelessly lost. I don't know how long I'd been out here, but it must have been weeks, as I had lost almost a third of my body weight. I was down to 63 pounds. My hair was so matted and dirty I must have smelled like a skunk. I was living under bridges, in concrete culverts, in drainage tunnels, anywhere I could find warmth and shelter. And I had just had a litter of puppies. I know, because I was still full of milk, and my nipples were huge. What happened to my puppies? I miss them so much.

Then one day I was walking aimlessly along Highway 331 near Defuniak Springs, Florida when a truck, with writing on the side, stopped on the other side of the road. A man with a uniform got out and went to the back of his truck. He pulled out a long pole with a round attachment on the end. I wasn't scared and for some reason, I didn't run away. He came across the highway with the pole toward me. Maybe he had some food? I looked up and he seemed kind enough and talked very calmly. He said, "Come here, boy," even though I clearly wasn't a boy. Then he reached out the pole and put the round "noose" around my head. When he tightened it around my neck, I panicked. I tried to run away but I couldn't – he had me tightly in his grasp. I was scared enough as it was, but when he led me across the highway and lifted me into the back of his truck, I *really* got scared. He loaded me into a cage and off we went.

A short time later the truck stopped and the man got out. He led me into a building with many other cages. I was put into a large one and was able to move around slightly. But soon the man came back with a bowl of food and put it into my cage. I gobbled it down in just a few bites. Then he brought me a bowl of fresh, cold water. Ah, it tasted so good. I fell asleep for the night thankful I had just had my first real meal in what must have been weeks.

The next morning, after making some phone calls, the same man came into the building where I was being kept and led me out of my cage and onto the back of his truck again. This time he didn't have to use the pole with the noose on the end, as I began to trust him and went willingly. He put me back into the same cage in the back of his truck and off we went.

We drove for a while, then we entered a gravel road. As the truck slowed, I looked out and saw a sign that read, "Alaqua Animal Refuge." This would become my home for the next two months. And so began the first chapter of my new life with Mister Dan.

Alaqua Animal Refuge

Alaqua Animal Refuge is located about five miles east of Freeport, Florida just off Highway 20. I would soon learn that it is the premier no-kill shelter serving the Emerald Coast, which is what they call the area where I live, due to the beautiful emerald green waters of the Gulf of Mexico. Alaqua provides protection, shelter and care to animals in need, and boy was I in need! It is a full-service animal adoption center as well as a peaceful, proactive animal welfare advocate through educational outreach and community programs. Alaqua is such a special place, not because of its facilities but because of its humans. I found that out immediately as soon as I was lifted out of the back of that kind man's truck that day in May 2016. The humans that I met are all caring, loving professionals who dedicate their lives to helping the animals like me that they receive. They are not only a home for rescue dogs and cats, but also have horses, rabbits, pigs, goats, chickens and roosters, and a variety of other farmyard animals. Alaqua provides respite for over 350 animals at any given time. Since its founding year in 2007, Alaqua staff and volunteers have helped find homes for more than 15,000 animals, with over 100 adoptions completed each month.

The first human that I met at Alaqua was a beautiful girl named Miss Alissa. She had long blonde hair, with purple on the end. The next week Miss Alissa would have long blonde and green hair, then it would be blue, then back to green, then maybe just her natural blonde. Each week I was excited to see what color Miss Alissa's hair would be. It didn't matter what color her hair was. What did matter to me was that she was the kindest, most loving human I had ever met. After she gave me a big hug, she said, "Cmon girl, let's show you your new digs." She led me to a kennel with a chain-link gate. Once inside, I could see there was a doggy door that led out to a large run where I could exercise. Inside the building was a bed all set up for me, a bowl of food, and a water bowl. It was air conditioned and a large fan blew cool air to protect us from the hot Florida sun. In the building I was in there were four other kennels, each set up the same as mine, with its own outdoor run and indoor sleeping quarters. In all, Alaqua has six buildings each with five kennels, so they can accommodate 30 dogs at one time. Since my time there, they have added another whole building and, when necessary, can even set up kennels to house dogs in the barn. There's a whole separate building to house cats, aptly named "The Cat House." Don't get me wrong – I like cats. But I'm sure they wish they were dogs. That first night at Alaqua in my cool bed with plenty of food and water, I thought I had died and gone to heaven. At least that's what it felt like compared to what I had just been through.

The next morning I met another wonderful human named Miss Reca. She was the vet tech for the Alaqua veterinarian, Dr. Amy Williams. Miss Reca led me up to a trailer with a sign on the outside that said "OR." Inside I met Dr. Amy. She is so kind and gentle and has the face of an angel. Miss Reca and Dr. Amy estimated that I was about seven years old. They did some tests on me and determined that I had heartworm. When I heard that word, I shuttered. Many of my friends have died of heartworm. Miss Reca started me on heartworm meds and gave them to me every morning for the next month. After she led me back to my kennel, she put a sign on my gate, I assume to let everyone know I had heartworm. Then a stranger came, also very nice, and walked me a short distance. As it turned out, I would be walked by wonderful volunteers twice each day, once in the morning and once again in the afternoon. Many dogs who have regular homes don't get that much exercise. Because of my heartworm condition, I could only be walked a short distance and very slowly. When a dog with heartworm gets excited or walks a long way, he can increase his blood flow and the heartworms can go directly to the heart, which is usually fatal. So for the first month or six weeks at Alaqua, until my heartworm was gone, I had to take it easy.

The next morning after she gave me my heartworm meds, Miss Reca again led me back up to the OR. She and Dr. Amy lifted me up onto a metal table. I felt a prick, but it didn't hurt. Then the room started to spin and everything went black. The next thing I knew, I was staring up at Dr. Amy's angelic face. As she cradled my head in her hands, she said, "There girl, you're all 'fixed'." "Fixed?" I didn't know I was broken. I don't know what she did, but that day everything changed. I looked at boy dogs differently than I ever had before. Oh, I still wanted to play with them and be their friend, but something changed. And the strange thing is, they looked at me differently too. It used to be where the boy dogs would all come around, have their fun, then they'd be gone, off with all the other girl dogs. They didn't care about my feelings and didn't give a hoot about my emotional state. And certainly none of them were interested in any type of long-term commitment. I understand that some human males act just like dogs. If you're a human female reading this and you can identify, maybe you, too, should come out to Alaqua Animal Refuge and get "fixed" by Dr. Amy. It's so freeing!

The next morning a new human came to walk me. I was a mess. I had heartworm, I was sore from my surgery, I was way underweight, and I must have looked pitiful with my matted and nasty fur. But he looked at me with sparkling eyes and a smile. He must have seen what I could become, not what I was at that moment. He introduced himself as "Dan" and entered my kennel. I sat and looked up at him as he fiddled with my harness, trying to figure out how to put it on me. With an anxious face I looked at him and said, "You know, Mister Dan, I really, *really*, have to go, but I'll wait here patiently till you figure that thing out." After what seemed like an eternity, he finally harnessed me up, attached the leash, and off we went. As soon as I got outside, I squatted. Ah, the pause that refreshes.

We started off on our walk. We went slowly, and he let me sniff everything. I love to sniff. Most dogs do. You see, our sense of smell is our strongest sense by far. I can smell something way sooner than I can see it or hear it. Unlike a human, who has about 10 million sensory receptors in your nose, dogs have anywhere from 200-300 million! And we don't exhale through our nostrils. We inhale through our nostrils, but exhale through the sides of our nose. So we can inhale a breath, hold it, process it, and inhale another before we exhale the first. I digress. As Mister Dan walked me that first day we met, I felt something different on the other end of the leash from the other volunteers I had met. He petted me on the head as we walked, and I snuggled closely to his side. I could tell he saw something in me that I couldn't even see in myself. As we walked back to the kennels, I started feeling a bond with this human that I had never known before. He put me into my kennel and as he closed the chain-link fence gate, I looked out at him and with the saddest brown eyes I could muster I said, "Where are you going, Mister Dan? Don't leave me here!" But he left. After his shift was over, he came back! He opened the gate and sat with me in my kennel for a long time, just petting me and telling me how beautiful I was. Was he going to become *my* human?

A few days later, Mister Dan returned, but it wasn't during his normal shift for walking dogs. He brought someone with him. After we got harnessed up and he attached my leash, we walked out of the building together and standing right outside was one of the most beautiful human females I had ever seen! She was short and had shoulder-length blonde hair and a gorgeous face. She introduced herself as Miss Bev. Was this Mister Dan's wife? Mister Dan is semi-handsome, but how did he end up with this beauty? She was way out of his league. She took my leash from Mister Dan and off we went, the three of us. I walked between the two of them and just like Mister Dan had done, Miss Bev petted my head as we went. I tried to snuggle up close to her as we walked. Even though several other humans had come to see me that week, not volunteers but humans from the general public, these two were different. I felt such a closeness to them both. After Mister Dan led me back into my kennel and removed my harness and left, I laid down to rest. I could only dream that this would be the family that would adopt me and take me to my forever home.

As I said, my hair was still matted and nasty, but that week I had been taken to the "grooming station." There a wonderful young human named Heather looked at me with sad eyes and said, "Girl, the only thing we can do with you is start over." She took a pair of clippers and started to shave my fur coat. She started behind my ears and shaved me completely from my neck to my hiney, including my legs and paws, leaving only the hair on my head and ears, and on my tail. She just brushed out the tangles in my tail. Normally, you never shave a double coated dog completely. Some humans do this on purpose, thinking they're helping their dog make it through the heat of the summer, like here in Florida. But our undercoat actually acts as an insulation against the heat, and the hair follicles keep us cool. But in my case, Miss Heather had no other choice but to shave everything off, as there were mats and tangles she just couldn't get out. Miss Heather was a professional groomer and volunteered her time one day a week at Alaqua. She became a friend of Mister Dan's and would end up being my permanent groomer, where she grooms dogs in her garage grooming setup.

I felt totally naked. The unexpected black spots that Great Pyrenees have on their skin were totally visible, usually hidden and never noticed under our white coats. As Miss Heather led me back into my kennel, the other dogs laughed. She said, "Don't worry, girl, it will all grow out again. It may just take a couple of months." That it did, and more.

Mister Dan came to walk me the next week during his normal shift. At first, he didn't even recognize me in my totally naked state. But he soon understood that Miss Heather did the only thing she could by shaving me completely. As he entered my kennel, he had a sparkle in his eyes. I thought, "What's up?" After our walk, he led me back into my kennel and left, smiling like a kid in a candy store. As it turned out, he would head immediately after his shift to the office and meet with Miss Kelby, the adoption counselor. With excitement in his voice, he told Miss Kelby he wanted to adopt

Jaynene. That is the name Alaqua gave me when I arrived. You see, when a stray dog comes into the refuge, if it has no collar, chip, or ID of any kind and they don't know its name, they pick a random letter of the alphabet and name every dog coming in that day with that letter. The day I arrived was a "J" day so I became Jaynene. I know, that's a stupid name and makes no sense, but more about my real name later. Miss Kelby looked up from her computer and sadly told Mister Dan that there had already been two applications put in on me. They must have been the "other" humans from the general public that came to meet me a few days earlier. Mister Dan left, completely heartbroken and thinking that our future together would never be. Then, two days later, Mister Dan got a text from another Alaqua staff member, Miss Bonnie, who had taught Mister Dan how to work in the "puppy zone," which he did for over a year. Her text read, "Dan, both applications on Jaynene fell through. Call Kelby!" Mister Dan would say later that God just wanted me to go home with *him*, and He cleared the way to make that happen. He called Miss Kelby, filled out the application she emailed to him, sent it back, and the rest, as they say, is history. A sign was put on the outside of my run that said, "Approved Application" to let everyone else know I was "taken." Since I wasn't well enough to go home with Mister Dan for another two months, little did I know then what my future would hold.

As the weeks passed, I started feeling a lot better and was gaining weight. I was up to 73 pounds and finally Miss Reca no longer had to give me my heartworm meds, as I was totally cured. I was wanting to play with the other dogs in the play yard after my walks, which were longer now, just as long as my other friends. Then it finally happened. The day came that I had been waiting for my entire life.

It was Friday morning, July 15, 2016, a day that will live in my memory forever. Miss Kelby came to my kennel after the volunteers had left and I had my morning walk. She had a brand new harness, a cool purple one, and a new leash. She put the new harness on me by slipping it over my head and snapping the strap under my belly and behind my front legs. Then she attached the new leash onto the ring on my chest and led me out of my kennel, which would be for the last time. As we approached the office, I could see Mister Dan and Miss Bev standing on the porch just outside the front door. They were beaming! I came to them and wagged my tail excitedly, and they both petted me all over. Then Miss Kelby took Mister Dan's phone and snapped pictures of me between him and Miss Bev. Then Mister Dan said, "Let's go, girl, let's get out of here." Was this really happening? Was I going home? They led me to their minivan and opened the back tailgate. I jumped in and we started to drive away. I had a bittersweet moment. As I watched Alaqua disappear in the rear window, I thought about all the incredible humans I had met there. All the volunteers who walked me were wonderful. Dr. Amy and Miss Reca saved my life. But most of all, I thought about Miss Alissa. She showed me what the love of a human can mean to a dog. She has a thankless job, cleaning out poop from dog runs and disinfecting them all day long. But despite all of that, she loved me and she loved all my friends. After reading Mister Dan's first book, *IT TOOK A DOG*, by Dan Holmes, available on Amazon, I think she understood how important her life is and she got to see "the big picture" by the end of his book that she probably doesn't get to see very often. She reintroduced me to the love of a human. I will never forget Miss Alissa, purple hair and all.

And so as Alaqua became a dot on the horizon, I was glad to be leaving. Alaqua is not a place you want to live forever. But they had given me my second chance at life. There were so many of my friends still there who I hoped would soon be as lucky as me. I laid down in the back of the van and drifted off to sleep. My dream had come true. I really was going to my forever home.

Going Home

It was about twenty minutes before we pulled into a circular driveway and stopped. I got up. The tailgate of the van opened and I hopped out with my new leash and harness still securely attached. OMG! This place is *huge*. I never lived in a house so big. For the last two months I was in a tiny room with dogs on either side of me. Mister Dan led me into the front door. He closed the door and removed my harness and leash. He snapped a new pink collar around my neck, pink to show everyone that I was a girl. I started to sniff everything. Mister Dan showed me the living room, then we went into his bedroom and huge bathroom and walk-in closet, which were all carpeted. Then I discovered the toilet room just off the master bath. This little room had ceramic tile and became one of my favorite rooms. I'll describe why in a few minutes. Then we stopped by the den, where I'd spend many hours making sure Mister Dan got it right while typing my book on the computer. Into the kitchen we went. At meal times this was the place to be, especially when Miss Bev was cooking chicken. I learned the word "chicken" soon enough, as Miss Bev cooked *a lot* of chicken! I would sit and look up at her with the most pitiful face I could muster, so she often gave me a piece. Down the stairs we went into what Mister Dan called his "man room." There was his flat screen TV with six Klipsch surround sound speakers, the best speakers on the planet, according to Mister Dan. I loved sitting down here while Mister Dan watched TV, especially when he sat on the floor with his back against the recliner so I could lie down and put my head in his lap while he petted me. Down the hall were two more bedrooms and a bathroom, but I seldom went down there, as both bedroom doors were always closed, I guess to keep my dog hair out of them.

Back up the stairs we went and into the final room in the house, the laundry room. This room, just off the kitchen, is where Mister Dan expected me to spend most of my time. I had other ideas. In addition to the washer, dryer, and a second refrigerator, Mister Dan had bought me a new food bowl and a smaller water bowl. He went to Lowe's and thoughtfully purchased a plant stand that raised my food bowl over a foot off the ground. This was really nice because as a big dog, now I didn't have to stoop down so far to eat out of a bowl on the floor. That's why you humans use forks and spoons. Without them, you, too, would have to lean down and eat your food right off your plate. How would you like it?

Then Mister Dan smiled and introduced me to what he thought would be my new dog bed. Right next to my food and water bowls up against the wall was this rectangular beast with green canvas stretched across PVC pipes which raised it about six inches off the ground. Then he had bought a large fleece blanket which covered the entire area. I looked up at Mister Dan and barked, "Mister Dan, do you have $#*! for brains? Do you really expect me, a double-coated Great Pyrenees living in Florida, to sleep on that? C'mon, man!" No way, Jose. I'm sleeping wherever I want, most likely on the cool tile floor. The only thing I used that dog bed for was to take some kibble in my mouth from my food bowl, turn and drop it on the dog bed and eat it from there. I think Mister Dan got the message, as I saw him loading it into his car about a week later on the day he normally walks dogs at Alaqua. I think one of my friends out there is stuck with it now.

As soon as we got home, right after our tour of the house, Mister Dan started a naming contest, as he thought the name Alaqua had given me was just as stupid as I did. He texted my picture to both his sons and their wives. After some suggestions came back from Scott with names referring to various aspects of the Pyrenees mountains from which my breed originates, Lauren, Scott's wife, texted back, "How about ELSA?" That was absolutely perfect! For you humans that are over 60 or have lived your lives in a cave, Elsa is the beautiful white snow queen from the Disney movie "Frozen." When it was released, "Frozen" was the highest grossing animated film in history. It made more money than "The Lion King," the "Toy Story" movies, you name it. Every kid under 10 knows who Elsa is – and every kid's Mom – especially since "Frozen II" was released last November. Mister Dan's 8-year-old granddaughter Maddie dressed up as Elsa for Halloween a few years before. And when we'd go out for a walk and a kid would come up wanting to pet me, the next question after "Can I pet your dog?" was always "What's her name?" When Mister Dan told them, there'd be an immediate connection, like "Oh yeah, Elsa." And it didn't take more than a few weeks for me to learn my new name. So thank you Lauren for the perfect name.

That same afternoon Mister Dan and Miss Bev took me to the vet. Dr. Scott Harris and his son Jason, who also graduated from the University of Florida Veterinary School, like his dad, and will no-doubt take over the business as Dr. Scott eases into retirement, checked me over thoroughly. I weighed 73 pounds and had a slight ear infection, so they gave me some drops in my ear and some pills, and wanted to see me back in two weeks. They also decided on my diet, and since Mittens, Mister Dan's last dog, had lasted 17 years on Science Diet, a dry dog food that Dr. Scott recommended, they decided that's what I'd eat. Two weeks later when we came back, I was up to 78 pounds. Now I weigh 90 pounds and I'm livin' the good life. When we left the vet's office after that first visit, Dr. Scott looked at me and said, "Girl, you hit the jackpot with these guys." Now I don't know who rescued who that day, as Mister Dan thinks I rescued him.

After we got home that night and it was time for bed, I sauntered into the toilet room, that tiny room off the master bathroom. This became one of my favorite rooms in the house, primarily because it has a cool tile floor to sleep on and it was pitch dark with no windows. I especially like to go there and hide during thunderstorms (there and the walk-in shower). Like a lot of dogs, I hate thunderstorms, probably more than a lot of dogs because I was forced to live outside in them when I was lost. Also the fourth of July is my least favorite holiday, followed closely behind by New Year's Eve. Why do humans have to be so loud during these times? But I digress. The toilet room was so small that when I wedged myself between the toilet and the wall, there was barely room for anyone else. And being the old human that he is, Mister Dan has to get up several times during the night to use the toilet room. When I was in there, he had to be careful. The first time he flushed the toilet that night, I jumped up and ran away. I just knew God had broken his promise about never destroying the earth again by flood. I thought the whole Gulf of Mexico was coming down on my head. But I soon realized that even with my head under the tank, the water would stay there and I'd be safe. So I got used to the toilet being flushed and didn't budge. This created a real dilemma for Mister Dan and at night when I was in the toilet room, he gave up and trudged down the hall to use the other toilet.

On our morning walks we always go down the street by the house of Mister Grant and Miss Amy, friends of Mister Dan. Mister Grant was a tremendous athlete in high school and actually starred on the first (and only) football State

Championship team that Niceville High School ever won in 1988. He went on to play college football, and came back to Niceville and taught and coached there until he became a big shot Principal at Destin Middle School. Miss Amy still teaches at NHS. Anyway, after his first book, *IT TOOK A DOG*, by Dan Holmes, available on Amazon, was published, Mister Dan stopped one Saturday morning and gave a copy to Mister Grant and Miss Amy. After reading it, they discovered Mister Dan's dilemma with the toilet room. So about a week later, they showed up at Mister Dan's door with a gift. It was a night light. This evil little contraption hangs over the side of the toilet, and when it's pitch black and senses motion, a little tube that points down into the toilet lights up the entire toilet bowl, first red, then blue, then green, then yellow, then white, then back to red again. The first time he used it, Mister Dan laughed like a hyena. But this thoughtless gift emboldened Mister Dan. Now he uses the toilet room at night even when I'm in there. If he misses left, I'm safe, but if he misses right, it's all over but the cryin'. Lucky for me this dastardly night light has accomplished its purpose and we haven't had any accidents. But it still makes me nervous. Thanks a lot, Mister Grant and Miss Amy, for your warped sense of humor.

Occasionally at night, after they crawl into bed together, Mister Dan and Miss Bev wrestle. I can always tell because a unique scent fills the air. On these nights, it seems like Mister Dan gets up fewer times during the night, and he gets a *really* good night's sleep. In my humble opinion, Mister

Dan and Miss Bev should wrestle *every* night. That way, Mister Dan would have more energy to play with me the next day after getting such a good night's sleep the night before. For some reason, I'm not sure why, I don't think Miss Bev agrees with me. Maybe she should go out to Alaqua and get "fixed" by Dr. Amy.

23

Vision

Just before Mister Dan and miss Bev brought me home from Alaqua, they flew to Colorado Springs to visit their youngest son Mark, his wife Jenny, and their grandkids. They flew through the Dallas airport and when walking from one terminal to another on a long, almost deserted, hallway they came upon a woman with a Great Pyrenees. They stopped and talked, and Mister Dan told her he was soon to be a Great Pyrenees owner. She was there with her dog as a therapy dog team. They talked about how great our breed is, and as she left, she gave Mister Dan her dog's business card. It had a picture of the dog on one side and information about her on the other. Mister Dan thought that was interesting, a therapy dog at the airport. He remembered this, and it would become key to our story later on, as you'll see why.

Mister Dan had retired almost a year before we met, so unlike his other dogs that he had while he was working, he had time to spend training me. Of course, he didn't consult me about this training, but he knew, as I do and all dogs do, that the common perception that you can't teach an old dog new tricks is totally false. All you need is treats, lots and lots of treats. I like to think I can do anything if there's a treat involved. "Treat" is one of the first words I learned from Mister Dan. Not content with trying to train me himself, he enrolled us in a dog obedience class with a local dog trainer about a month after he brought me home. This place is called "Pets Behave" run by Miss Debbie Revell, which is only a few miles from our house. The thing I liked about Pet's Behave is that all their training is based on positive reinforcement. They never use spiked collars, hitting, or yelling. Positive reinforcement means, yep, you guessed it, TREATS! Mister Dan learned that a couple of the tests we would take later on did not allow treats. So most of the time, he would provide me with treats for just about everything I did. But later, rather than withholding treats altogether (which he knew wouldn't work with me), he would trick me into thinking he had one. So I learned I had to obey every time just in case. Except for our first visit, where I learned I'd be in a class with about five or six other dogs which I had to ignore, I loved Pet's Behave. Of course, I wanted to play with all the other dogs, and they wanted to play with me. But again, using treats, all the humans learned to keep their dogs close to them in their own little space. We attended a six-week class of beginning obedience training, and Mister Dan was so impressed with my progress, he enrolled us in a second six-week class for intermediate obedience training. The thing is, we only attended class once a week for about an hour. So most all of my training was done at home with Mister Dan after he learned the techniques to use from the classes.

The three basic commands that I learned first were "sit," "down," and "stay." Most well-behaved dogs know these three commands. As a bonus, Mister Dan added shake hands, and he *thought* he taught me my left from my right. But I just learned that if I raised one paw when he said "shake" and it didn't work, then I'd raise the other and there was the treat! "Sit" was simple, as Mister Dan would put the treat in his hand above my head and I could do nothing but sit and look up if I wanted it. "Down" was almost as simple, as Mister Dan would lure me to lay down with a treat placed near the floor in front of me. But "stay," now that was a challenge! After I learned "sit" and "down," Mister Dan would put me in one of those two positions, then he would put his hand in front of my face and say "STAY!" But then he would step backward about ten paces while still facing me. He still had the treat in his hand, so naturally I had to get up and follow him to get it, right? WRONG! He would say "NO," then usher me back to where I was and start over. This went on and on. He'd say "STAY," walk away, and I'd get up and follow him. After several sessions of this over a couple of days, I got really ticked off. So finally after "STAY" and he walked away, I knew I wasn't getting the treat if I followed him, so I just laid there. To my surprise, Mister Dan came back to me, praised me, said "good girl, Elsa," and wala, gave me the treat! What just happened? All I did was……STAY! So that's what "STAY" means. OK. I think I got this. Mister Dan did it again, and again I "stayed," got my treat, and everyone was happy. Mister Dan would walk backwards but further away, and I learned that if I continued to "stay," I'd get rewarded. Then he changed things up. He would turn his back on me and walk away as if he wasn't coming back, but I learned if I just laid there, he always returned. Finally, and this was the hardest part about "stay," he'd put his hand in front of my face, say "STAY," then disappear, like behind the wall or into the next room. But again, if I was just patient, which is totally counter to this Great Pyrenees' disposition, I'd be rewarded with a treat when Mister Dan finally reappeared. I eventually learned his "release command," which is "OK." That means I can go back to doing what I was doing before, and in the case of "STAY," it meant I could get up and come to him to get my hard-earned treat. This all sounds very exhausting, and it was.

As difficult as "stay" was to learn, what was even harder was "leave it." Mister Dan would put a treat on the floor, and as we passed by it, he would say "LEAVE IT!" Of course, I would stoop over to get it. But Mister Dan pulled on my leash as I went for it and we continued walking. Realizing that I wasn't going to get the treat anyway with a tight leash, I learned to just ignore it. After that, Mister Dan would loosen up the leash so I could reach the treat, but as we passed by the treat, he would command "LEAVE IT," then he would put his foot over the treat so I couldn't get it. Finally, I learned that if I just ignored the treat on the floor as we passed by, I'd get another one he always had in his pocket later on. So after several frustrating days, I finally learned what "leave it" meant. Mister Dan also used this command when he wanted me to ignore other dogs that we passed by on our walks, which was even harder than ignoring a treat on the floor!

But nothing compares to the ultimate dog command "COME!" I reckon most dogs intuitively know and understand this command, but few of us actually obey it. Or more accurately, *hear* it! You see, like all dogs, I have 18 muscles in my ears, but usually only one is engaged. The other 17 stay in hibernation and "selectively" hear whatever they want to hear. They'll wake up if it's a squirrel, rabbit, or particularly, another dog. But to hear "COME" for a dog is like a human hearing another human babbling incoherently and you just ignore it. To his credit, Mister Dan took his training from our obedience classes and taught me "COME" by buying a 15-foot leash, which he attached to my collar when we were out in the back yard. He would tell me to "stay" and he would walk backwards as far as the leash would reach. Then he would say "COME," and pull me towards him, finally giving me a treat when I arrived. Then he removed the leash and I would "come" to get my treat.

After six weeks of beginning obedience training and six more weeks of intermediate obedience training, Mister Dan signed us up for three more weeks of training in preparation for what is called the American Kennel Club (AKC) Canine Good Citizen Test. This test is very similar to the test they give for therapy dogs. We passed this test with flying colors, and I did it without the hint of even one treat! I got a ribbon and I was so proud.

You see, Mister Dan started to have this thought, and later would call it a *vision*, that God put in his head, and then his heart, that together, we could become a Therapy Dog Team. I had no idea what a therapy dog was, but he explained that it was totally different from a service dog. A service dog is very special, and I have the utmost respect for them. Service dogs are protected by the Americans with Disabilities Act (ADA), which became law in 1990. The ADA is a civil rights law that prohibits discrimination against individuals with disabilities in all areas of public life, including jobs, schools, transportation, and all public and private places that are open to the general public. A service dog works with just one person and is individually trained to do work or perform tasks for that individual with a disability, usually to help them navigate basic life skills. Service dogs are highly trained animals that are covered under the ADA, and therefore must be allowed in public areas, such as an office building, schools, restaurants, etc. even if state or local health codes prohibit animals on the premises. It takes usually a minimum of 18 months and sometimes over 2 years to train a service dog, depending on what they're being trained for and to whom they will be assigned. They are working dogs and wear a vest that says, "Service Dog," and under that label usually the words, "Please Do Not Pet." Service dogs can be valued as high as $25,000 or more, and often times a non-profit, such as Wounded Warriors, will pay the fee to provide a service dog to a soldier with post-traumatic stress disorder (PTSD), for example. Whenever I see a service dog Mister Dan has trained me to "leave it" and let him work.

So what is a therapy dog? Therapy dogs work with a variety of humans in differing environments, and usually just try to make them feel better. Therapy dogs have been known for years for their healing power, as the medical community can attest. Many hospitals have therapy dog programs. Although trained, tested and registered, a therapy dog does not receive nearly the level of training as a service dog. Like any dog except a service dog, we are not allowed in restaurants unless it's a dog-friendly restaurant, such as Boshamps Seafood and Oyster House in Destin, named by combining the names of the owner's three labs, Bobo, Otis, and Shug along with his initials. I love going to Boshamps with Mister Dan. Unfortunately, some therapy dog owners try to bring their dog into a restaurant by telling the staff they are a therapy dog, and many humans don't know the difference between a therapy dog and a service dog.

But once again, I digress. Where did Mister Dan get the idea that I could be a therapy dog? Well, I suppose it started as soon as he brought me home. My coat had grown out from being shaved at Alaqua and after a few weeks I was back up to my normal weight of about 90 pounds. I was, quite simply, gorgeous! Any Great Pyrenees owner knows how beautiful our breed is when properly groomed, and Mister Dan brushed me almost every day, which I loved. Whenever Mister Dan took me on walks I was like a human magnet. Humans of all shapes, sizes, ages, male or female (but particularly female) would come up to me and tell me how beautiful I was and asked if they could pet me. Mister Dan met more beautiful females because of me. And I love being petted. It's about my favorite activity. The very first time Miss Bev walked me by herself, a little human about 9 or 10 years old saw us from the window of his house and ran outside all the way to the street to ask if he could pet me. Whenever Mister Dan took me out to a public place, like the open-air mall called Destin Commons near our home, I always seemed to draw a crowd. One week in October Mister Dan took me to Seaside, a dog-friendly beach community about 30 minutes away, and it was mobbed with humans on fall break from school. It took almost an hour for us to walk one block for all the kids that wanted to pet me and hear my story. They have a three-tiered drinking fountain for dogs near their town square with a bowl on all three levels, the lowest for small dogs, the middle for medium-sized dogs, and the top tier for us big dogs. Of course I had to take a drink out of all three. As a crowd gathered to watch this, Mister Dan told them I was looking for the one with the gin in it, whatever that is.

So it became clear to Mister Dan that because I am so beautiful and have such a calm demeanor, especially with little humans with whom I'm very patient despite their poking me in the face and pulling my tail, I would be a good therapy dog. During our training at Pets Behave, Miss Debbie gave Mister Dan the name of a human who lives in Freeport, Florida as a contact for therapy dog training. Miss Debbi Cole is the Northwest Florida Chapter Director and a Licensed Evaluator and Instructor for Intermountain Therapy Animals (ITA), which is headquartered in Salt Lake City, Utah. Mister Dan would later claim that he thought ITA was the best therapy dog organization on the planet! Miss Debbi has three therapy dogs of her own, all standard poodles, which she also breeds. Mister Dan called Miss Debbi and she was excited that he was interested in pursuing therapy dog work. She was having two full-day seminars at her home, for humans only without their dogs, in January 2017. One was a day-long training class for therapy dog teams, with a thick workbook and a required written test at the end that the human must pass to become a therapy dog handler. The other was a day-long training class to qualify for R.E.A.D.®, which stands for Reading Education Assistant Dogs at school. Miss Debbi explained that R.E.A.D.® is the first and foremost program that draws on the power of therapy dogs (and occasionally cats and bunnies) to help little humans improve their reading and communication skills, while falling in love with books. It's been growing around the world since November of 1999 when ITA launched it in Salt Lake City. More than 6,000 therapy teams have trained and registered with the program. They currently have teams in 26 countries and regions outside the United States, so it's truly an international program. Basically, you take the dog into the school, and the little human reads to the dog, one-on-one, for about 20 minutes. It's a brilliant concept, as it turns education on its head. The child becomes the teacher, and teaches the story to the dog. It's designed for first, second, and third graders who are having difficulty with their reading. They gain self-confidence, and when they become better readers, they typically do better in math, science, and all their other subjects. Although Mister Dan didn't know if we'd ever do R.E.A.D.® together, he signed up for that seminar as well. Of course, there was a cost for each of these classes.

Before Mister Dan actually took these classes and paid his money, he wanted to see if I would be good for this kind of work. So he called Miss Angela, the Activities Director at The Manor in Bluewater Bay, a nursing home and rehab center only about a mile from our house. Mister Dan had been to The Manor a number of times visiting people he knew going through physical therapy, or people from his church who were now permanent residents there. Miss Angela asked that we come over and she'd give us a tour of the facility. We did that the next day and after meeting me and showing us all around, we went back to Miss Angela's office. She immediately asked, "Well, when do you want to start?" Mister Dan said, "Whoa, wait a minute. We're not even registered as a therapy dog team yet." He thought maybe we'd go one time. Miss Angela said she didn't care about that and that we would do fine. So they set up a schedule for us to come in every Tuesday from 10:00-12:00 in the morning.

The next Tuesday in early December we came for the first time. It seems I became an immediate hit. As I approached people in wheel chairs, their faces would light up. One gentleman was steeped in dementia and kind of out of it. But when he reached down to pet me, suddenly he snapped back into reality and was there, fully in the present and cognizant of his surroundings. Almost everyone we visited thanked us for being there, and we occasionally got comments like, "You've made my day." Mister Dan learned to respond to that comment by replying, "Hearing you say that just made MY day." And it did. We went home that day from The Manor and I could tell Mister Dan had changed. He sat down in his chair in the living room, with me lying beside him, and he talked to me, as he often does. Dog lovers understand. He said, "Ya know, girl, I worked 43 years for the Air Force, and not once in all those years did I ever come home from work feeling like I feel right now." I think he felt like we actually made a difference in someone's life that day. If we didn't "make their day," at least we put a smile on a lot of faces. Mister Dan claims that he didn't do anything, and that it was all about me, Elsa, the dog. He believed that he was just along for the ride. But I knew better. I knew I couldn't do anything without Mister Dan, my owner, my handler, my best friend. And he couldn't do anything without me. We were a team, and one couldn't do anything without the other. That day Mister Dan knew that this is what he wanted to do. He would attend those seminars, study, and hopefully one day become a registered Therapy Dog Team with me, Elsa, the therapy dog!

The next Tuesday that we showed up at The Manor, as soon as we got to the first hallway, Tonto, a big guy on staff that we had met the previous week, yelled at Mister Dan from way down the hall. "Dan, Dan." Mister Dan looked around and thought oh no, what did I do? He said, "Make sure you see Miss Gracey in room 102 before you leave. She wants to see Elsa." And that's how it went all morning. A few people remembered Mister Dan's name, but *everyone* knew me, Elsa. I think the physical therapists and nurses on staff were just as excited to see me as were their patients. One particular nurse, a beautiful tall human named Miss Christy Brooks, was my favorite. She had two dogs of her own and always had bone marrow treats in her cart she gave me. Since I learned to sit in dog obedience training to get a treat, I would approach Miss Christy and her cart and immediately sit and look up in eager anticipation until the treat came. Then, when she ran out of treats or, heaven forbid she forgot treats that day, I would continue to sit and look up, putting Miss Christy on a guilt trip. Every time Miss Christy bent down to pet and hug me, I would nuzzle up next to her and bury my head in Miss Christie's chest or armpits. Mister Dan was downright embarrassed. But having dogs of her own, Miss Christy was a great sport about it. Then one week something was different and the close nuzzling didn't happen. Mister Dan and Miss Christy discovered that it was her perfume! When Miss Christie wore my favorite perfume, I would go nuts over her. But when she changed to another scent, I was much less affectionate. Did I mention a dog's sense of smell?

The next month, in January 2017, Mister Dan drove out to Miss Debbi Cole's house and with several other handlers went through the therapy dog training. Thankfully he passed the written exam at the end. The next week he returned for the R.E.A.D.® seminar. Finally, the big day arrived at the end of January. Mister Dan and I went over to K9-5 Daycare and Training in Santa Rosa Beach, Florida where we were evaluated together as a therapy dog team. The AKC Canine Good Citizen test prepared us well. I did great, but Mister Dan was a wreck! Miss Debbi and Miss Nancy Bown, the owner of K9-5 who was the other evaluator, told Mister Dan, "Son, you need to chill out. You're making your dog nervous." He was so afraid we might not pass, but not to worry, we did! After our test, the next week they met us at Brookdale, a nursing home at Grand Boulevard right off Highway 98, for a practical examination to observe us in a nursing home environment. We did fine there, as I knew we would, as we'd been to The Manor a half dozen times by then. Mister Dan received his paperwork and we were officially registered as a Therapy Dog Team with ITA on February 2nd, 2017. We automatically received a $2 million liability insurance policy to cover any incidents that might occur. Since its founding over 25 years ago, ITA has never had one claim against their insurance for any of the thousands of therapy dog teams registered with them, which is a testament to how strict, well trained and professional their therapy dogs are. Mister Dan's *vision* ever since he brought me home had become a reality.

Opportunity Knocks

Now that we were a registered Therapy Dog Team, Mister Dan was looking for other opportunities besides just The Manor at Bluewater Bay to take me and serve together. Mister Dan was looking to "enlarge our territory," in human speak, but we didn't know quite what that would look like. Mister Dan found that if you are open and receptive, sometimes opportunity finds you.

About a month after our therapy dog test, Mister Dan was working out at the Bluewater Bay Gym. In walks a gal he hadn't seen for several years, but he knew she was back in the area. Her name is Miss Christine, a tall, slender beautiful blonde, and she's a lawyer. Miss Christine and Mister Dan go way back. She actually worked for him at Eglin AFB when they were both on active duty in the same squadron. Miss Christine was an Air Force Academy graduate, so after her five-year commitment, she got out and went to law school at Samford University in Birmingham, where Mister Dan's youngest son Mark got his undergraduate degree. She had returned to Niceville and went back into the Air Force Reserves, eventually retiring from the Judge Advocate General's (JAG) office at Eglin as a full Colonel. Mister Dan was happy to see her again and catch up. He told her about me and just becoming a therapy dog team. Miss Christine's eyes lit up. She said she was now a prosecuting attorney with the District Attorney's office working at the Emerald Coast Children's Advocacy Center (ECCAC) in Niceville, a non-profit, prosecuting child abuse cases. She told Mister Dan they use therapy dogs at the ECCAC, and urged him to call Miss Jacqui at the center. Miss Christine is a dog-lover with two dogs of her own, and Miss Jacqui, a mental health therapist, has two therapy dogs she used to bring to work every day, although one, Riley, retired from therapy dog work, as he's 13 years old. I was fortunate to meet both Riley and Cody before Riley left.

Mister Dan called Miss Jacqui and she was anxious to meet us. Later that week we met and she was excited that we agreed to commit one day a week to come into the ECCAC. We started the very next week. The ECCAC is set up like a house, but they don't house little humans there overnight. Instead the CEO and her assistant's offices are downstairs as soon as you enter the "house," and back rooms are set up as offices for the three mental health counselors and other staff that work there. Upstairs are offices for Miss Christine and her legal team, plus one other lawyer, and officers who work for the Florida Department of Children and Families (DCF). The entrance to the facility has a cypher-locked door to control entry and right off the hallway is a room set up like a living room with toys, puzzles, and activities that kids can occupy themselves with while waiting to speak with a counselor.

Mister Dan takes me there for two hours every Monday afternoon, generally when new intakes arrive, in the living room downstairs to welcome the little humans and the parent, guardian, or social worker that brought them in. It seems that 90% of the ECCAC caseload is for physical or sexual abuse. So the vast majority of the kids we see are deeply wounded humans. It is our job to welcome them and make them feel safe. We want them to trust us, and hope that their time petting me will allow them to relax and know that they can open up and trust the counselor that they will see that day. Mister Dan soon discovered that the counselors, legal beagles, and staff love to see me as much as the kids do. After all, they have a tough job hearing heartbreaking stories day in and day out. As soon as we arrive in the parking lot, I know where we are. I jump out of the car and make a beeline for the front door, because I know what awaits me inside – TREATS! It seems every human in every office has treats for me. As soon as we get inside, I immediately go to Miss Julie's office, the CEO, and sit and wait for her to give me the large Milkbones she keeps in her office. One day Miss Julie's door was closed. Where was she? Didn't she know this was Monday afternoon and I'd be here for my treat? I sat outside her office for about ten minutes waiting for Miss Julie and my treat, but she never showed up that day. Rats! After Miss Julie and Miss Angie's offices, I pull Mister Dan up the stairs and to Miss Gail's office, one of Miss Christine's assistants in the legal department. I used to enter her office and sit and alert right on her top left desk drawer. This is where Miss Gail kept her treats. Unfortunately, Miss Gail retired last year and now when I go to her office, her door is always closed. I finally realized I wouldn't see Miss Gail anymore. How thoughtless of her to retire! Then it's off to Miss Tiffany's office, the paralegal right next to Miss Christine's office, and her top drawer. And so it goes. Everyone who works at the ECCAC, it seems, looks forward to Monday afternoons so they can see me.

At that point Mister Dan and I worked two days a week. Mister Dan still volunteered at Alaqua walking dogs in the mornings on Monday, and when he got home I would be all over him, sniffing him and wondering who he'd been "seeing." Was he cheating on me? Monday afternoon's we would be at the ECCAC and Tuesday mornings we'd visit The Manor at Bluewater Bay. That left the rest of the week open. A few months after working just two days a week, Mister Dan remembered the lady at the Dallas airport with her Great Pyrenees therapy dog. He thought that certainly our little Destin-Fort Walton Beach airport (airport code VPS because it's actually located in the town of Valparaiso, Florida) isn't as big as Dallas, but it always seems crowded, especially in the summer months during tourist season when millions of humans come to our beautiful beaches. Besides, with the addition of the low-cost airline Allegiant, the Destin-Fort Walton Beach airport has been designated the fastest growing airport in the country! Would VPS benefit from a therapy dog team? Mister Dan emailed the Deputy Director of Airports, Mister Mike Stenson, and offered our services. About a week later, Mister Mike emailed back and seemed very interested. He wanted to meet me and asked that we come to his office for what we thought was an "interview." Mister Dan wasn't worried. He just figured if he kept his mouth shut, I would be so irresistible Mister Mike couldn't say no. We arrived at the airport at the appointed time and Mister Dan rang for the elevator to access the administrative offices upstairs as Mister Mike had directed. Miss Lori Fox, the airport's executive assistant, answered the call, saw Mister Dan and me on the closed circuit TV camera by the elevator door, and enabled power to the elevator so we could come up. Miss Lori turned out to be a real sweetheart with two dogs of her own, petted me and immediately made a fuss over me. She showed us to Mister Mike's office, and he met us at his door. Before we even had a chance to enter his office, he said, "Come with me." He escorted us out to the main terminal and watched Mister Dan and me "work" the room. Mister Dan would walk up to a passenger waiting for his flight, with me in tow, and say, "Hi, my name's Dan and this is my friend Elsa, and we're here just to say hi to everyone at the airport today." Mister Mike watched us for about 30 minutes, and I guess that's all he needed to see. He led us back to his office, and again, before we even went in, he said, "When can you start?" So much for our "interview." Mister Mike took us to the office next door and we met Mister Tracy Stage, the Airports Director. Mister Mike introduced us as the airport's new therapy dog team! He then took us over to the security office and Mister Dan arranged to come back a few days later, by himself, without me, to begin the badging process. Miss Sirah Masters, the Regulatory Specialist for the airport, escorted us downstairs and out through the exit to the unsecure area. Mister Dan would meet with her and Miss Tiffany Wills, the airport Security Specialist, a few days later to get fingerprinted, photographed, and start the background check with the Federal Aviation Administration (FAA). On our way out of the airport that day, we met a real nice cop at the podium they have set up for security just outside the secure area and he told us a good time to come would be on Fridays about noon, as several flights arrive at that time, which means there are a lot of humans waiting for flights to depart. Also Friday is a fairly heavy travel day. So Mister Dan arranged with Mister Mike that our schedule would be once a week on Fridays from 12:00 noon till 2:00 PM. About a week later, Miss Tiffany called Mister Dan that his badge had come in, and he just needed to come over and take a security test before it could be issued. After passing the test the next day, he was issued an all-access badge to all areas of the airport. Under his name were the words "Therapy Dog Handler." Now when we get to the airport each Friday, Mister Dan just rings for the elevator, Miss Lori lets us upstairs, and we can go ourselves out to the terminal, thus avoiding TSA screening each week.

One other thing Mister Dan remembered about the gal and her therapy dog at the Dallas airport was that she had a "business card" for her dog which she gave to Mister Dan when he left. Miss Jacqui at the ECCAC also had business cards for both of her therapy dogs. So he thought, what the heck, he'll make one up for Elsa. Like the ones he had been given, he made up mine to include my mug shot on the front and some tidbits about me on the back, as well as his cell phone number and email address. Mister Dan would come to find out later that he was glad he included his contact information on my business card. Mister Dan originally ordered 250 cards, thinking they would last a good year. Well, with meeting hundreds of people at the airport each week, and giving out so many of my cards to humans who were particularly interested in me, he went through that batch in about three months! He's now on his second batch of 500 of my business cards!

A couple of months after starting at the airport, Mister Dan got a call from his mentor and ITA rep Miss Debbi Cole asking if he would like to start R.E.A.D.® with me at Freeport Elementary School. It was already January of 2018, and usually the program starts at the beginning of the school year in September and runs through early May. But Miss Debbi, who had been doing R.E.A.D.® at the elementary school, switched to Freeport High School working with ESE kids and other humans with special needs. So that left an opening for a team at Freeport Elementary. Even though we were a qualified R.E.A.D.® team, it had been almost a year since he had taken the R.E.A.D.® seminar at her house, and Miss Debbi was conducting another one the next week, so Mister Dan sat in on that one as a refresher. We started R.E.A.D.® at Freeport Elementary the next month and went until early May. What a great time I had listening to kids read to me. Sometimes they just wanted to pet me and play with me on the floor, but Mister Dan told them they had to read to me first. I always got two treats from each student, one at the beginning before they sat down to read to me, and one at the end of their reading session. At the end of the semester, each of my five students got a certificate of completion with my picture on it, a bronze medallion they could wear around their neck, again with my picture on the back, and a picture book story of me. Mister Dan had taken pictures of me and sent them to the R.E.A.D.® organization, which made up a separate, personalized hard-back book for each kid. It was entitled "Elsa Goes to School," by Elsa Holmes. So this is not my first rodeo at being an author! It would have a picture of me sleeping on the floor, and might say something like, "Elsa always gets a good night's sleep before she goes to school. Did you get a good night's sleep last night?" Then a picture of me eating my "breakfast" and the caption saying, "Did you eat a good breakfast before you came to school this morning?" It would go on like that with me arriving at school, reading my favorite book, and finally reading with that particular student to whom the book would be presented. At the end of the semester R.E.A.D.® even presented Mister Dan a book from Elsa to Dad.

Freeport is a small town in Northwest Florida, and the school was almost 25 miles from our house. It took us almost a half hour to drive there. So Mister Dan figured if we were going to continue in the program, he'd like to do it at a school much closer to our home in Bluewater Bay in Niceville. In fact, Bluewater Elementary School is less than a mile from our house. The problem was, our school district, the Okaloosa County School District, did not approve the program for their schools. Never mind that it was approved and working in our neighboring school districts, including Santa Rosa County and Walton County, not to mention all over the United States and in 26 countries outside the United States, including Canada and Mexico. I won't go into the details here of what Mister Dan went through in trying to get R.E.A.D.® approved in Okaloosa County. He does that in his first book, *IT TOOK A DOG*, by Dan Holmes, available on Amazon. Suffice it to say, the previous Superintendent of Schools and her staff were not in favor of the program. So, for whatever reason, the disapproval of R.E.A.D.® in our local district got Mister Dan to thinking. We have a private Christian school only about five miles from our house in Niceville, Rocky Bayou Christian School. Mister Dan called them, then Mister Dan, Miss Debbi and I were invited over. We talked to them and they were excited that we were available for the program at their school. Of course they didn't have to go through the bureaucratic nightmare that is Okaloosa County Schools. We started R.E.A.D.® at Rocky Bayou Elementary in September 2018 and completed our first year there in April 2019. At our little graduation ceremony in April, attended by not only my six students but their entire class, one of my students came up to me afterward, hugged me and buried her head in my neck, and started to cry. She wasn't going to get to read to Elsa anymore.

Not to be deterred with Okaloosa County, after the previous Superintendent of Schools was fired, as were some of her staff, Mister Dan saw an opportunity. The new Superintendent was Mister Marcus Chambers, a previous acquaintance of Mister Dan's. He contacted Mister Marcus and asked for a meeting to discuss R.E.A.D.®, which was never able to be arranged with the previous Superintendent. Mister Marcus immediately agreed, and a meeting was set up in early September 2019. Mister Dan contacted Miss Debbi after he set up this meeting, and she also wanted to attend. Of course, Mister Dan asked that I be allowed to come along as well, and I did. I think just my presence made a difference, because the meeting went very well, even though I slept at Mister Marcus' feet through most of it. Mister Dan told me afterward that he was very hopeful, because Mister Marcus seemed very supportive of the program. Little did he dream that only ten days after their meeting, R.E.A.D.® was approved in the Okaloosa County School District! Now R.E.A.D.® is being conducted at nine elementary schools in Okaloosa County by seven different R.E.A.D.® teams. Mister Dan and I do R.E.A.D.® at Plew Elementary in Niceville, only about four miles down the road from our house, every Wednesday. I'm so glad Mister

Dan persevered and never gave up, and after two and a half years, finally was successful in getting R.E.A.D.® approved in Okaloosa County Schools.

With the addition of the airport and R.E.A.D.®, I was working with Mister Dan four days a week. Even in the summer, when R.E.A.D.® had taken a break, we were invited by a therapist at the Rehabilitation Institute of Northwest Florida in Destin to come to their facility once a week to visit their patients. She had been working weekends at The Manor and saw one of my business cards and contacted Mister Dan. Did I mention that Mister Dan was glad he included his contact information on my business card?

We take off on Thursdays. Mister Dan knows I'm getting older, and I guess he doesn't want to burn me out. I'm sure, even though he won't admit it, he could use a break too. Mister Dan knows that the first and foremost thing you learn in therapy dog training is that the handler must be an advocate for his dog. The handler must do what's in her best interest. After two hours at the airport, for example, I'm whipped, and I start to lie down at people's feet. Even if we haven't visited everyone we'd like to in the terminal, we call it a day and go home. After spending two hours at The Manor feeling the loneliness of the older humans who live there, I go home and crash and burn all afternoon on Tuesdays. So Mister Dan figured I need one day during the week to just be a dog. Indeed we had enlarged our territory.

The Incident

I t's not hard to train a dog to be a therapy dog. You just have to know the basic commands that I learned at Pet's Behave of "sit," "down," "stay," and "come," as well as a number of other observations they look for during testing. The dog must be at least 18 months old, and it's better if it's two or older, as you want that puppy behavior out of them completely. The human must have owned the dog for at least six months. Mister Dan learned that my demeanor was key to me becoming a therapy dog. If a dog is high-strung or jumpy, he best look for another line of work. Some dogs would make coffee nervous. Just the opposite, I'm so laid back that at night, before he goes to bed, Mister Dan has to coax me over and over if I'm asleep or just chillin' to go outside to the bathroom. When I finally do get up, we go downstairs and he lets me out in the back yard without a leash and encourages me with "Let's go potty Elsa, cmon, let's go, hurry up." Of course, I take my good ole time, explore, and sniff extensively as Mister Dan continues to encourage me from the back door. Finally, I squat. Mister Dan goes crazy! You'd think the human just won the lottery. "Way to go Elsa. Good girl. Atta way. Yeah Elsa." I'm thinking, "Calm down, dude, all I did was pee." Then he'd encourage me to hurry up and come back inside, forgetting that the Great Pyrenees hurries for no human. After sniffing some more, I finally meander back inside. Yep, I was born to be a therapy dog.

As far as staying in Mister Dan's yard, I've come a long way since he first brought me home. Within the first week, however, I escaped twice. The first time, a visitor came to the door, and when Mister Dan cracked it open, I made my break. I ran down the street, and Mister Dan ran after me. I'd stop, look back, then let him get within about ten feet and I'd take off again. This was a fun game that we played for almost a mile. Then the human who had come to the door had driven his pickup truck after us and caught up. He stopped, got out, and he and Mister Dan cornered me. Game over! The second time I got out Mister Dan cornered me in a neighbor's yard. It was into the lake or back home. Since I'm not a good swimmer, with relatively short legs for my large body and a heavy coat, I chose Mister Dan over the lake. He soon learned that we Great Pyrenees are wanderers, and we love wide-open spaces. Maybe that's how I got lost in the first place. In any event, Mister Dan never put up a fence in his back yard, thank goodness. I hate fences. He considered installing one of those underground electric fences that shock the dog by its collar if it tries to get out, but thankfully realized that they use these fences as negative reinforcement, which is never a good idea.   So Mister Dan worked with me extensively to stay in his yard without fences, underground or otherwise.

Mister Dan has a deep back yard that backs up to a lake, which is bordered on the other side by a golf course. It's very peaceful and quiet at night. There are not many distractions, so now at night I like to just lie in the grass out back and I'll stay put. One evening I was out there and some human started fishing from the golf course on the other side of the lake. I went crazy and started barking and carrying on. That's MY lake and that guy was not to be intruding. You see, we Great Pyrenees' territory is whatever we can see out in front of us, regardless of where the property line ends. It was much more difficult for me to learn to stay in our front yard, as there are many distractions with joggers, golf carts, cars, and most of all, people walking their dogs. But now, after several years, I've learned to stay put in our front yard as well.

Mister Dan and I go for a walk twice a day, once in the morning for about seven-tenths of a mile, and once in the evening about a mile and a half. So I get my two miles plus in every day. Whenever we go on a walk, we often meet other dogs, as we live in a very dog-friendly neighborhood. There are no sidewalks bordering our streets so usually Mister Dan takes me over to meet the other dog. I love to play with other dogs, especially Jackson, a boxer/pit bull mix that lives down the street and is almost as big as me. He's my absolute favorite!

One day we were walking in the afternoon and we saw a woman, whom we had never seen before, pushing a baby carriage and leading a rather large dog. It looked like a retriever mix and probably weighed about 75 pounds. Mister Dan took me across the street to see if we could meet. I approached this dog, smiling with my tail wagging, but the other dog wanted nothing to do with me. The dog lunged at me, baring its teeth, and growling ferociously. It's a good thing Mister Dan had me on short leash. Otherwise, this son of a bitch (and I mean that literally) would have been dead meat! I thought, "Your day's coming, #$$*0!&." Mister Dan walked me back across the street without saying anything to the woman. In the days ahead, we would see this woman several more times with her baby carriage walking her dog. Her schedule must have been similar to ours. Each time Mister Dan put himself between me and the dog across the street and tried to calm me down as we passed by. I didn't forget.

One day I was outside in the front lying peacefully on the cool concrete driveway while Mister Dan was trimming bushes on a ladder with hedge clippers. Mister Dan didn't normally let me out in the front yard, untied, as I hadn't figured out yet that I needed to stay put. But he assumed he could intervene if he needed to. Suddenly, I saw the woman with the baby carriage and her unfriendly dog approaching on the other side of the street. They were behind Mister Dan and he didn't see them coming. I bolted. Before Mister Dan could jump down from the ladder and drop the hedge clippers, I had run across the street and attacked the SOB. By the time Mister Dan got across the street and grabbed my collar, we were locked in mortal combat. Somehow I got my teeth locked inside his mouth. Mister Dan pulled and pulled and it must have been ten seconds before he got my mouth and teeth out of the other dog's mouth. The woman was screaming and our yelps were deafening. Mister Dan dragged me across the street while apologizing profusely to the woman, saying I've never acted like this before. They kept on walking and Mister Dan pulled me into the house. He slammed the door and went back outside to work. He was furious! But what did he expect? This vicious mutt was intruding upon MY territory, I felt threatened, and I would have none of it! I laid down on the cool tile floor. There was a bit of a stinging in the side of my neck, but since I couldn't reach it with my tongue, I just ignored it. As Mister Dan worked outside, all he could see was dollar signs. He just knew this woman was going to come back to the house that night with her husband. After all, she knew where we lived. Mister Dan was ready to tell her he'd pay for any vet bills if her dog was injured. She'd threaten to sue and report this to the authorities. He was afraid our days as a therapy dog team may be over.

It was over an hour before Mister Dan was done with his yard work and calm enough to come back inside the house. When he got inside, I remained lying on the tile floor at the end of the hall afraid of what he might do to me. But as he approached me, he noticed a big red spot on my neck – apparently it was blood! I had been bitten. He pulled my fur back to examine my wound. It was a puncture wound but no big deal. Since he didn't know if I needed stitches, he called the vet after cleaning the blood off my fur with a wet paper towel. Dr. Scott said to bring me in right away.

When we arrived at the vet's office, the vet tech shaved my fur off from around my wound and Dr. Scott and his son Jason were both there and examined me. They decided my wound did not require stitches (like I said, it was no big deal), but they gave Mister Dan some antibiotics to give me for ten days in case that other canine's rabies shots were not up to date. Then Dr. Scott had a heart to heart talk with Mister Dan. He said he should report this to the health department, but that if he kept me essentially quarantined for the next two weeks, he'd forego the report. Mister Dan was not to let me out of the house except to do my business. "But," I thought, "what about our TV gig?" That upcoming weekend we were both to be on a fund-raising telethon with the Emerald Coast Children's Advocacy Center (ECCAC) in South Walton County on their local TV station. I was going to be a TV star! But Dr. Scott said no, absolutely not. This dog was not to be out in public that soon. We left, and even though Dr. Scott was not going to report the incident, I was bummed.

When we got home, Mister Dan called the ECCAC and told them that I had been bitten by another dog and we had to cancel out of the telethon Friday night. They were concerned for me and said they could easily fill our 20-minute time slot and not to worry. What Mister Dan didn't tell them was that I was the aggressor, I had attacked the other dog, and if he'd only let me go, that other mutt would be crossing the rainbow bridge by now. When Miss Bev got home from work, Mister Dan told her what had happened and they both awaited the inevitable knock on the door that evening. It never came. Thank goodness – that woman's dog must not have been injured, and it was most probably me who got the worst of it. We have never seen that woman again. She must have found another route to walk her baby and her #$$*0!& dog.

A few days later, against Dr. Scott's orders, Mister Dan and I went to the Destin dog park. He wanted to see how I would react around other dogs. Mister Dan stayed closer to me than usual, and as I approached all the dogs at the park, I wagged my tail and was ready to play. I was my old self and I had a blast. This incident and one idiot was in my past and was not going to have any effect on my friendliness toward other dogs.

Ever since "the incident" took place, I've come a long way in learning to stay put in the front of our house. But I don't think any amount of training would have prevented what happened that day. I had had a bad experience with this dog before, I was threatened, and I was bent on protecting my territory. Now I pretty much stay put in the front yard even if another dog walks by – any other dog, that is, except Jackson. I love Jackson, he's my bud. We love to play together. If Mister Steve walks by with Jackson, I'm there. We used to have a neighbor next door who had three dogs, but Mister Tom moved away. I especially loved Finley, who's about 50 pounds, and we used to play together all the time. We could get pretty rough with each other, but I always let up after a few minutes and we'd lie down together to rest. So despite the incident, I'm still as dog-friendly as ever.

I think Mister Dan learned a lot about me that day, and he also learned a lot about my breed, the Great Pyrenees, the best dogs….ever! We were originally bred in the Pyrenees mountains in Spain and southern France, hence the name. We're called mountain dogs. We actually have two dew claws on our hind legs, the upper dew claw to help us make it through the snow – brilliant! God knew what he was doing when He made our breed. We are sheep dogs and blend in with the flock. As gentle as we are, we have been known to attack bears, wolves, coyotes, or anything that would threaten the flock. There are shepherds in the Pyrenees today who say they couldn't have a flock without the dog. In the U.S. today we're used as livestock dogs, protecting not only sheep and goats but hens and other farmyard animals as well. In the 14th and 15th centuries, French kings would have a Pyrenees stationed at the entrance to their castle, not only to protect the king and his family, but as a sign of royalty. We really are regal-looking dogs. So we have always been known to be extremely protective, and I think Mister Dan now understands that my natural instincts boiled over that day. The only time I bark is when the doorbell rings, or someone knocks on our door. Someone who's up to no good would probably think twice before coming through that door when they hear my deep, loud, menacing bark. But as soon as Mister Dan or Miss Bev lets that person in the door and say "It's OK, Elsa" I'll wag my tail and, if they pet me, will immediately be that person's best friend. I think my forever family knows they're safe with me.

At the Airport

Of all the venues that we visit each week on our therapy dog visits, the one where I meet the most humans is undoubtedly the Destin-Fort Walton Beach airport. I'm sure we meet well over 200 in the two hours that we spend there each week. We have been welcomed with open arms by the entire staff. Mister Tracy, the Airports Director, has treated us like one of the family and part of the team. His Deputy Director, Mister Mike, has been more than accommodating and is the one we can thank for bringing us on board. But my absolute favorite is Miss Lori, who enables the elevator to let us upstairs to the administrative offices each week. She is such a kind lady and has two dogs of her own. We talk about her dogs and visit for a few minutes before venturing out to the terminal. She always makes a fuss over me and pets me behind the ears, which I love. I'm sure her own dogs love her too. Miss Tiffany and Miss Sirah in security have been just wonderful to us, as have all the humans on staff selling things throughout the terminal.

People ask Mister Dan, "Why the airport?" Well, that question was answered the very first week we visited after his security badge had been issued to him. We approached a young girl, maybe 20 years old, who was absolutely terrified. An elderly lady was sitting next to her, got Mister Dan's attention, and then left her seat, as if to offer it to him. As we got nearer this girl, I saw that she was almost in tears. She had only flown once in her life, from Boston to get down here, and this was her second ever flight. Mister Dan sat down next to her and I sat down at her feet. Mister Dan talked to her for a while and as she petted me on my head, I could feel the fear just melt away, if only for a few minutes. I knew right then why we were there and the value of having me, a therapy dog, at the airport – to meet and comfort humans just like her.

Even if we don't often meet humans who have a fear of flying, and even though I've never flown on an airplane myself, Mister Dan tells me that air travel can be stressful. It's usually a long day, with getting to the airport before your flight, getting through security, and getting to your destination after you land. And that's if everything runs smoothly. If your flight is delayed, with the possibility of missing a connecting flight, or if it's canceled altogether, well that's just the last straw. Besides, who wouldn't want to see a beautiful Great Pyrenees like me while waiting in an airport?

I feel like a rock star when we go to the airport. Everywhere we go in the terminal people are scrambling to pull out their cell phones to take a picture of me. Mister Dan knows who the star is, and he's just along for the ride. One time, a lady felt sorry for him and actually took *his* picture! After telling me how beautiful I was, she looked at Mister Dan and said, "You're cute too!" I usually try to "pose" for my pictures. Mister Dan pulls out a treat, holds it up and out of view of the picture and I'll raise my paw. It makes a cute pic with my red scarf visible as I'm looking up. One particular day we approached a young girl and her husband. She was fumbling through her purse, but instead of her phone, she pulled out a bona-fide camera – a nice one, big, expensive-looking. She said she was a photographer and would Mister Dan mind if she took some pictures of Elsa. She actually wanted to go to a hallway where there were no people so she could get a clear background. After snapping away, we walked her back to her seat with her husband and Mister Dan gave her one of my business cards. She thanked Mister Dan and me and we left. A little while later that same day we came upon a family with five kids, all under the age of about nine. The husband was very cordial and made sure each of his kids asked if they could pet me before approaching. I laid down on the floor and all five kids came over. One was at my head, one was on my butt, and several in between. I loved it and soaked it all in. Mister Dan noticed the parents seemed relieved to have just a few minutes to themselves without having to watch all these kids.

Two days later Mister Dan told me he received an email from Jessica Williams, the gal with the camera. Her email read, "Hi, Dan! My husband and I met you at The Destin Airport last week and I snapped these shots of sweet Elsa. Thanks again for letting us pet her! It brightened our day." I perked up when I heard "sweet Elsa!" The two photos she sent were in black and white, which were absolutely stunning with my white coat. One was a close-up of my head with a hand petting me, and the other was of both of us, Mister Dan in the background out of focus (as it should be) with the sharp focus on me. They were so professional-looking that Mister Dan had both pictures enlarged to 5 by 7's and he has them framed on his dresser to this day. The next day Mister Dan got another email, this one from a man we had obviously met that same day but are embarrassed to say we don't remember at all. Mister Dan must have given him one of my business cards, because he emailed Mister Dan the following: "Dan: Made it back home, to the California Central Valley, and while unpacking discovered Elsa's business card. I just wanted to drop you a short note and tell you how much I enjoyed your introduction on Friday, March 2. Of course, I really enjoyed the interaction that Elsa had with the little kids that you visited with after you left me. How does Elsa put up with all that manhandling?! I had a smile on my face the entire trip to Dallas thanks to you. Hopefully it won't be too long before I make it back to the Emerald Coast and see y'all again. Sincerely, Larry Zerwig." Mister Dan responded to his email and thanked him for his kind note, and attached the two pictures Jess had taken that day. On another day, we visited with two teenaged girls for a while. After their petting me was over, they walked away and I heard one girl say to her friend, "This is the best airport *ever*!"

After visiting for two hours on another Friday we were leaving the airport and were in the main lobby on our way out. A beautiful woman approached with two friends and they were dragging their bags, so they were most likely about to check in. (Did I mention Mister Dan has met more beautiful females because of me?) This woman looked at me, then looked at Mister Dan and exclaimed, "Oh my God – that's the most beautiful dog I've ever seen! Can I per her?" Mister Dan smiled and said, "Sure, that's what she's here for." She bent over, cupped my head in her hands, and gave me a big kiss on the side of my face. I loved it! But when she stood up, Mister Dan looked down and I apparently had a huge red lipstick mark all over my white nose. Such is the life of a rock star! As soon as we got outside, Mister Dan annoyingly took his handkerchief out of his back pocket and tried to wipe the lipstick off of my face. When we got home, Miss Bev was in the kitchen. She's usually the one to do the laundry. So Mister Dan took the handkerchief out of his pocket, and as a preemptive strike, waved it in front of her face and said, "She kissed the *dog*, she kissed the *dog*!"

Our Destin-Fort Walton Beach airport has probably become the fastest growing airport in the country due to Allegiant Airlines. Allegiant is a low-cost carrier that has designated our airport as their hub. They have added a myriad of flights to a number of different cities. In the summer during tourist season, the downstairs "A" terminal, from which Allegiant flies, has become crowded, at least on Friday afternoons when Mister Dan and I are there. It takes us almost an hour to get through that terminal before even heading upstairs to the "B" terminals out of which United, American, and Delta flies. One day after visiting scores of humans downstairs, we finally made it to the end of the terminal, where there was this little girl, maybe about a year old, as she was barely walking, playing on the floor with her mother. There were several flight attendants sitting on chairs against the window. As I approached this little girl, the mother gazed up at Mister Dan with a very troubled look on her face. She said her little girl was deathly afraid of dogs, particularly big dogs. I was very cautious, but I smiled at her and as I got closer to her, the little girl started crawling toward me. She didn't seem frightened at all. I stopped and sat, and the little girl started to pet me. After a while, I laid down. The toddler began to stroke my face, then started to crawl on top of me, finally burying her head in my side. I was in heaven! Her mother was amazed. She got out her phone and started to take a video. She said, "I've got to send this to my husband. He's not going to believe this!" She told us her daughter had never acted this way before around a big dog. She was thrilled. Of course the flight attendants sitting nearby also had to get some pictures of this adorable sight. As I got up to leave, the mom thanked us profusely and I couldn't help but think, "Well, that problem's been solved. Hopefully she'll never be afraid of big dogs ever again."

I see a lot of other dogs at the airport, probably too many. In fact, before they know I'm a therapy dog, people will ask Mister Dan if we're going on their flight, probably thinking they don't want to sit next to me, as I'll take up all their legroom. Mister Dan immediately tells them no, we live here, and we aren't flying anywhere today. Most of the dogs I see are small dogs, most in a portable kennel that people carry with them on the airplane on their laps. With all the other smells at the airport, with humans eating everywhere, I at times don't even smell another dog until we're right up on them. If another dog starts barking at me, we just leave the area to stop the commotion, even though it's not our fault. Every once in a while, I see a service dog at the airport. Mister Dan has the utmost respect for all service dogs, and whenever Mister Dan and I see one at the airport, we leave it alone and stay well away so he can do his work.

One day while at the airport we were walking down the "B" corridor upstairs and we saw a service dog. At least it appeared to be a service dog, as it had a vest that said "Service Dog." But Mister Dan noticed that the moniker "Please Do Not Pet" or "Please Ask Before Petting" was not written anywhere on the vest, as is usually the case with any service dog vest. We tried to keep our distance from this dog, as we usually do with any service dog, but the owner, who was a young strapping-looking dude with no visible sign of a disability, approached us with the dog. As he got close, he asked, "Is your dog friendly?" Mister Dan said, "Sure," and we started sniffing each other's behinds, as all dogs do to get acquainted. Then, much to my delight, this dog started to jump around as if to play. So I started to play, and we were having a great time with each other. Then Mister Dan told the guy we needed to get along, and as we walked away, the other dog barked – *loudly*! Then it barked again. His handler had to hold it back from following us – that dog just wanted to continue playing. Mister Dan was astonished. A red flag immediately went up. Something's not right here. Its behavior was like nothing he'd ever experienced before with any service dog we'd ever come in contact with. Service dogs just don't act like that. The more I continued to visit with other passengers, the more I could feel Mister Dan's anger welling up inside of him. I think Mister Dan concluded that dog was no more a service dog than I was. In fact, I was a lot better behaved than that "service dog." Mister Dan figured the idiot went on-line, ordered a "Service Dog" vest, slapped it on his mutt, and was probably using it to get on this flight. There are even on-line web sites where you can get "paperwork" for your "service dog."

As Mister Dan and I concluded our visits at the end of the terminal and we had to walk back past this dog, which was now lying in the middle of the hallway floor, Mister Dan wanted to confront his owner. He thought about the two questions that the ADA allows you to ask any service dog handler; that is, "Is the dog a service animal required because of a disability?" and "What work or task has the dog been trained to perform?" Mister Dan also wanted to ask for some ID or any paperwork on the dog. Whenever we're out together on a therapy dog visit, Mister Dan always wears his polo shirt with the TPC logo (Therapy Patient Connections, the local affiliate ITA group), and he clearly displays his ITA badge (or his R.E.A.D.® badge if we're at school). In addition, while at the airport, Mister Dan wears his airport security badge, which, under his name, says, "Therapy Dog Handler." Of course, I always wear my red scarf around my neck. Mister Dan decided to let it go and not make a scene, so he just put himself between me and the bogus service dog as we passed by.

A final note – if you're one of those "fakes" who try to pawn your dog off as a service dog, shame on you! You're screwing it up for every bono-fide service dog out there, and even us therapy dogs. Besides, misrepresenting a dog as a service animal is a crime. Unless you're going to a known dog-friendly restaurant, leave your dog at home when you go out to eat and don't try to cheat its way into a restaurant by telling the staff it's a service dog. This puts the business owner on the spot. Unfortunately, this has become all too common, and is detrimental to legitimate service animals.

In the Courtroom

Occasionally, when it's not too hot outside, Mister Dan will take me to one of our therapy dog sessions in his BMW with the top down. I take up almost the entire back seat, and love to just stand up and lean against the back of the seat with my face in the wind and my ears blowing in the breeze. I love it. And boy do I get some looks. A while back we were out and had stopped at a traffic light in the middle of Niceville. I looked back to see the young female driver behind us laughing and snapping away pictures on her phone through her windshield. Even though Mister Dan waved, he knew he was just the roadie chauffeuring the movie star in the back seat. Another time we were stopped in Destin, just as tourist season had started, and a whole carload of females pulled up next to us. One yelled out her window, "What a lucky dog." Mister Dan assumed she was talking about me having such a nice ride. I think I mentioned that Mister Dan sure has met a bunch of beautiful females since I came along. It seems like the female species make much more of a fuss over me than the guys do.

I've been on over 300 therapy dog visits (and counting) with Mister Dan. People ask him if there's one experience in all those therapy dog team visits that was the most impactful and stands out above all the rest. The answer is "yes."

About a month after starting at the Emerald Coast Children's Advocacy Center (ECCAC) in Niceville, I was upstairs one Monday afternoon visiting with the legal gals. After getting loved on by Miss Gail and then Miss Tiffany, I went into Miss Christine's office. She bent down to hug me, then stood up with a serious look on her face. She told Mister Dan she was prosecuting a sexual abuse case and would he consider being a therapy dog team with Elsa in the courtroom for the two girls involved when their case went to trial. Mister Dan told her we'd never done anything like this before, but we'd give it a try if she thought we could be of some help.

The case involved two sisters who were 18 and 20 years old at the time. I won't use their real names for privacy purposes, so I'll call the younger sister Anna and the older sister Lila. Anna was sexually abused by her step-father when she was only 10, 11, and 12 years old. Lila, although herself not abused, knew what was happening to her little sister toward the end. So why did it take so long for this case to come to trial? Because both girls were threatened by their parents, including their biological mother, who must have known what was going on, that if either girl said anything to anybody, it would destroy their family. Their parents would be thrown in jail and the girls would be thrust into foster care, never to see each other again. They held this lie over the girls for several years. Finally, after the family had moved to Pensacola, Florida, Anna, then 16, met a boy she could finally trust and confide in. She fell in love. When the boy broke up with her, she later said that it was the lowest point she had ever had in her entire life. She no longer cared about her family, and finally came forward and reported the abuse.

The parents of these two girls (their biological mother and the step-father) were a real piece of work. They had a son between them who was much younger than the girls, and the boy was autistic. He was 5 years old when the abuse was reported, and was removed from the parents' custody and became a ward of the state. While the investigation was on-going, the parents requested to see their son. A meeting was arranged and a social worker took the boy to meet with his parents at a Burger King in Crestview, Florida. In a lapse in judgement, the social worker left the boy alone with the parents while she went to the bathroom. When she came out, they were gone. The parents had kidnapped their son, got in their truck parked outside which was pulling a U-Haul trailer with all of their possessions, and took off. They were finally apprehended in Nevada. Both parents were extradited back to Florida and prosecuted, and the boy was put back into foster care. So both the girls' step-father and their mother were in prison at the time of their trial. Of course, the jury was never made aware that the defendant appeared in the courtroom directly out of prison, as his crime was totally unrelated to the sexual abuse allegation.

In order for Mister Dan and me to appear in the courtroom during the trial as a therapy dog team, Miss Christine knew she had to get permission from the judge ahead of time. The judge is in complete control and has the final say for anything that goes on in his courtroom. At the trial, Miss Christine anticipated that the defense would object to our being in the courtroom, claiming that it created an unfair advantage for the prosecution. That's exactly what happened, and the judge had to overrule the defense's objection, which he did. As it turned out, the judge that ended up taking the case was one that Miss Christine had worked with many times in the past, and he was a personal friend of Mister Dan's. His name is Judge Michael Flowers. Judge Flowers is a fellow-Christian, just like Mister Dan, and has been a long-time member of his church. What a coincidence – or was it?

It was in the spring that Miss Christine approached Mister Dan and me on this, and the trial kept getting continued and continued and continued, month after month. The defense was responsible for the delays, always asking for more documentation and continuances. I guess this is normal. Anyway, the trial date was finally set for December 2017. The girls were living in Atlanta at the time, and had to come down to Florida for the trial. Miss Christine asked that they come down a couple days early, which they did.

About a week before the trial, Miss Christine arranged to meet Mister Dan and me at the courthouse in Fort Walton Beach to show us around the inside of a courtroom, to give us the "lay of the land" so to speak. When we arrived, we had to go through security screening similar to that at an airport. When Mister Dan walked me through the metal detector, he forgot to take off my collar with all my metal tags on it. The metal detector blew up! Everyone kind of smiled and let us through. I guess they didn't think I was any particular threat. Miss Christine was already there to meet us, and took us upstairs to the only empty courtroom that afternoon. As it turned out, it was not the courtroom where our trial was to be held, but the layout was similar. We decided that a chair could be set up behind the witness box for Mister Dan, and he would have me on leash at all times. I would be in the witness box with each of the girls when they testified. There were small wooden doors, like a gate, at the rear of the witness box that would be propped open to allow me to enter. Mister Dan would be seated behind the witness box at all times, hopefully inconspicuously.

The day before the trial was to begin was a Monday, and Mister Dan and I were at the ECCAC that afternoon doing our thing with the kids in the downstairs living room/lobby. At about 3:00 PM Miss Christine walked into the center with both Anna and Lila. We met them downstairs, and then Miss Christine ushered us all upstairs to a conference room and closed the door. The girls' biological father, who lived in Kentucky at the time, was also there, having come down for the trial to be with his daughters. Miss Christine left us alone with the girls for over an hour. This was a brilliant move on her part. With the doors closed, Mister Dan dropped my leash and let me meet each girl in turn. As they petted and embraced me, Mister Dan told them my story, about being a rescue dog, a throwaway that nobody wanted. But look at me now! I was given a second chance at life, just like they would be given after this trial. This bonding time that the girls got to spend with me was crucial for what happened the next day.

I don't remember much about my past. That's because I don't live there. I live in the present, in the here and now. But the day of that trial, Tuesday, December 12th, 2017, is a day I will never forget. The opening remarks by both attorneys were to begin at 9:00 AM, followed by Anna's testimony, and then Lila's testimony. Since Anna's testimony was scheduled for 10:00 AM, Mister Dan and I got to the courthouse about 9:30 to ensure we had plenty of time. We walked through security, who knew me by this time, and upstairs. There was a very small room just outside the courtroom where all involved in the trial were "sequestered" until called into the courtroom. They had to bring extra chairs into the small room when we arrived, as there were both girls, their father, and several others associated with the trial. As it turned out, the girls' father was not allowed in the closed courtroom and stayed with his daughters in that small room throughout the trial. I laid down with the girls on the floor, who petted me and we got reacquainted while awaiting their turn.

At precisely 10:00 AM the door to the small room opened and the bailiff asked for Anna to follow her. We entered the courtroom, first the bailiff, followed by Anna, then me and Mister Dan. The bailiff led Anna to the witness stand, and Mister Dan led me behind the witness stand, passing directly in front of the jury. I could feel eight sets of eyes focused on me and I smiled as we walked past. But, for some reason, Mister Dan made it a point not to make eye contact with any of the jurors. He propped the wooden doors open behind the witness stand and I walked inside. Anna was sworn in, and after sitting down on the witness chair, I finally laid down directly behind the chair. Miss Christine would tell us later that because the witness stand had a solid wooden front and side (toward the jury) that nobody could see Elsa at all from the courtroom. But Mister Dan could see most of the jurors, so he assumed they could see him, and possibly some could even see me.

The questioning would begin with the prosecution, then would continue with the defense, and finally the prosecution could cross-examine at the end. Miss Christine started with some fairly benign questions, but as her questions became more personal, things got tense. Finally, Anna was asked to describe, in intimate detail, the things that her step-dad had done to her as the abuse got worse. At one point during her descriptions, Anna started to struggle, then completely broke down sobbing. At that moment, I knew she was in trouble. She needed me. I stood up, walked around to the side of Anna's chair, and buried my head in Anna's lap. As Anna's tears fell on my head and she stroked my ears, I felt Anna's pain. I took on her emotions, and I just wanted to be there for her. I wanted to take away Anna's pain so she could be free – free to gather herself and continue to recount her personal hell. When Anna finally was able to compose herself, I walked back behind her chair and laid down. This happened not once, but twice more, and each time I went to Anna's side to be there for her. Several times during her testimony, there might be an objection raised by one of the attorneys. When this happened, the judge would usually ask the attorneys to approach the bench. When they did, and there was a "break in the action" so to speak, Anna would reach down looking to pet me.

The last time Anna "lost it," Mister Dan almost did too. She described that when the abuse was at its worst, and the sex almost daily, she had a little dog that she went to. This dog was the only thing in the world she could talk to, the only thing she could trust, her only friend. Then the parents took the dog away. Hearing that, I was incensed. Mister Dan had to fight hard not to cry. He told me later that he couldn't imagine that happening to him, someone taking me away from him when he needed me the most. He fought back the tears with all his might, and it was all he could do to contain his emotions. He realized this was not about him and it was not about Elsa. The focus had to remain on Anna, and he couldn't let the jury turn their attention to him. Finally, Miss Christine's questions were over. Before the defense was allowed to proceed, Judge Flowers wisely called for a 10-

minute recess, to allow everyone a break, especially Anna and me.

When we reconvened, the defense attorney asked his questions. At one point, he intimated that Anna was having sex with her boyfriend when she was 16 and living in Pensacola. When he said this, Miss Christine was enraged. She jumped up and loudly said, "Objection!" The judge called both parties to the bench, and although I couldn't hear what he was saying, it appeared the judge was admonishing the defense attorney for this line of questioning. That had nothing to do with this case. It was obvious what he was trying to do. He was trying to put doubt in the jurors' minds about Anna's credibility. On her cross examination questions, Miss Christine skillfully put any of this doubt to rest.

Following her cross examination, Miss Christine thanked Anna and she was excused. Anna had been on the stand for an hour and forty minutes! It was 11:40 AM, and Judge Flowers adjourned the trial until 1:00 PM so everyone could take a break for lunch. Lila's testimony would take place right after we reconvened. The bailiff led Anna out of the courtroom, followed by me and Mister Dan. Mister Dan again avoided any eye contact with the jurors as we passed directly in front of them and I smiled. As we approached the prosecution table, Miss Christine was still standing, and her eyes met Mister Dan's. She smiled and as we passed by, she touched Mister Dan on the arm and I heard her whisper in his ear, "Thank you."

As soon as we got out of the courtroom, Mister Dan dropped my leash and gave Anna a big hug. He told her how proud he was of her and how courageous she had been. We walked downstairs and out of the courthouse. I was famished. Thank goodness Mister Dan took me to the nearest McDonald's, which was right down the street from the courthouse. In addition to his Big Mac, he also ordered two plain cheeseburgers for me. I guess he must have appreciated what I had just been through. He took our food back to the courthouse and we walked out to the Fort Walton Beach Fairgrounds, which are right adjacent to the courthouse. This is a big expanse of land, and we found some picnic tables under a pavilion where we went to eat. Mister Dan gave me one of my cheeseburgers and I gulped it down with one bite. I heard him say, "Dang, girl, you're gonna get sick! I don't want you puking all over the courtroom this afternoon." So he broke up the second cheeseburger into bite-sized pieces and fed them to me one at a time. We went back into the courthouse at 12:50 and upstairs to the small room outside the courtroom.

At precisely 1:00 PM the bailiff once again opened the door and asked for Lila. We entered the courtroom as before and Mister Dan led me back into the witness box, where I laid down behind Lila's chair after she was seated. Lila's testimony was not as emotional as Anna's, and it took only about 40 minutes. She did have to recount that when the family moved to Destin and lived in a hotel room together, she suspected what was going on with her little sister, especially since Anna was forced to sleep in the same bed as her step-dad. Finally, Lila was excused and we all left the courtroom. It was 1:40 PM. When we got back inside the little room, there were two more witnesses to testify that afternoon. One was a girl about Lila's age, who was a friend of the girls, and the arresting officer. There was no need for us to stay any longer, so we said our goodbyes. For the first time, I saw real emotion on the face of the girls' father, as he thanked us for being there. Anna and Lila gave me a big hug, and we left. I will never forget those two girls, their courage and bravery, and I don't think they'll ever forget me on what had to be one of the toughest days of their lives.

On the ride home, before I fell asleep in the back seat, I thought about what had happened that day. I had a new-found respect for prosecutors like Miss Christine who have to try these type cases day in and day out, and judges like Judge Flowers who have to rule on them. Recently when Mister Dan and I were visiting Miss Christine in her office, I was sniffing her bookcase looking for treats. It was filled with file folders. She told Mister Dan that each folder contained a separate case, and she now has 120 active cases. And that's just in one county, Okaloosa county, and just one prosecutor. Unbelievable!

When we got home, Mister Dan received a call that evening from Miss Gail, who was at the trial. She told Mister Dan that the witnesses had testified after Lila's testimony, and that the next day would be the closing arguments at 10:00 AM before the case went to the jury. Miss Christine had invited

Mister Dan to be there. He thanked her and hung up. I don't think Mister Dan thought very long about going. Like me, he had seen enough of the inside of a courtroom and didn't care if he ever went back. So he didn't go. But Mister Dan told me that if Miss Christine asks us to do this again, we probably should.

We found out the next day that Miss Christine had hit a "home run" in her closing arguments. She must have. After several hours of deliberation, the jury came back with the verdict – guilty on all four counts. Judge Flowers sentenced the defendant to life in prison without the possibility of parole on the first count, so I guess his sentencing on the other three counts was a moot point. It was a tremendous victory for us all, knowing this human will never again do this to another human.

Looking back on my experience in the courtroom that day, I tried to make sense of it all. How could one human do such terrible things to another human? Why was there such inhumanity of one human against his fellow human? Why can't humans treat each other like us dogs treat humans? It's really not that hard to show love and affection. For me, it just comes naturally. You humans could learn a lot from us dogs. As I drifted off to nap time on Mister Dan's cool tile floor, I was sad. For once, I was glad I was just a dog.

The Extra Chapter

This is the extra chapter. This is the chapter that Mister Dan never included in his first book, *IT TOOK A DOG*, by Dan Holmes, available on Amazon. That's because the events in this chapter didn't occur until after Mister Dan published that first book. I didn't want to write this chapter. Mister Dan didn't want to include this chapter either. But we both decided that as hard as it was, what happened last year, in 2019, and early this year, 16 months we would both like to just forget, was crucial to telling my story. What happened helped define who I am, and my story wouldn't be complete without it. So here goes.

It was a Monday in January. I knew it was Monday because Mister Dan, as he usually did, left to walk dogs at Alaqua right after our morning walk. But Miss Bev didn't go to work that day. Instead she left to go walk in a parade in downtown Fort Walton Beach with some of her friends from the college. When he got home from Alaqua and I finished sniffing the scents from all the other dogs he still carried, he told me we wouldn't be going to the Children's Advocacy Center that afternoon, like we usually do on Mondays, as it was closed for the Martin Luther King Holiday. Miss Bev came home from the parade and we had a leisurely afternoon. But something was off. Ever since Miss Bev got a phone call from Jenny, Mark's wife, on Friday, she and Mister Dan seemed concerned all weekend. Mark was sick, but they didn't know what was wrong. After dinner that evening, the phone rang and Miss Bev answered it. It was Jenny again. After she talked on the phone for a few minutes, she hung up, and she and Mister Dan sat down together on the couch. I was lying down in the living room close by. They held each other close, then, for the first time, I heard Miss Bev use the "C" word. Mark, their youngest son, 36 years old, married to Jenny for over 10 years with three kids, Maddie, seven, Will, five, and Anna, who just turned one, had cancer!

After they talked for a few minutes more, Mister Dan stood up and walked out of the room. I followed him. He went into their bedroom and as if he knew I was behind him, left the door open. He sat down on the floor with his back up against the bed. He looked at me, held out his arms, and I walked toward him. I buried my head in his chest and sat down on his lap. He held me tighter than he'd ever held me before. Then, he buried his head in my side and started to cry. He wept uncontrollably. I had never felt such pain. I had felt the loneliness from the older humans at The Manor. I had felt the fear from the little humans at the Children's Advocacy Center. And I certainly felt pain that day in the courtroom. But nothing compared to the pain I felt that night. This was personal. Mister Dan was my human, and I was his dog. We cried together on the bedroom floor that night for a very long time.

The next day, during our morning walk, Mister Dan talked a lot. But he wasn't talking to me. He was talking to Mister Jesus. When we got home, he took a shower and got cleaned up, then he came to me, snapped my red ITA scarf around my neck, and said, "You know girl, they say when you're feeling your worst, go out and do something for someone else. Let's go." We went outside and I climbed into the back seat of the car, and off we went. In just a few minutes we arrived at The Manor for our normal Tuesday visit.

Mister Dan smiled and joked with the staff and the residents during our visit that day, but I could tell he was distracted. He was thinking about Mark. About halfway through our visit, we came to Miss Angela's office. She wasn't in. As it turned out, she was home caring for her sick son. Finally, when we got to the long hallway where my favorite nurse hung out, I approached Miss Christy's cart and dutifully sat and raised one paw. She smiled and pulled out her bottom drawer and gave me my bone marrow treat. Yum! Then I looked up and raised my other paw, and she gave me my second treat. Mister Dan and Miss Christy talked for a short time, then Mister Dan said that since Miss Angela was out, there was something he needed to tell her so she could relay it on to the rest of the staff. Miss Christy saw the serious look on his face, and she led them into an empty room. I followed them. She closed the door and Mister Dan told Miss Christy about Mark. Miss Christy started to cry. She wrapped Mister Dan up in a big bear hug, and Mister Dan started to cry too. They hugged for a while, then Mister Dan told Miss Christy we wouldn't be visiting again for a while. She said she understood and that she'd pass this news on to the rest of the staff. As we walked away, Miss Christy told Mister Dan she would be praying for Mark and his family.

The last room we always visited at the end of the last hallway was the room of Miss Janice. She was such a kind lady, but she was so crippled with arthritis that she couldn't get out of bed and she couldn't even reach me to pet me. But she loved our visits and was always so conversant and positive. The month before, there was only one thing she told Miss Angela that she wanted for Christmas. Miss Angela emailed Mister Dan to ask for a picture of him and me. He sent her a digital photo, and the staff had it enlarged to a five by seven, had it framed, and gave it to Miss Janice for Christmas. This was her favorite gift that year, and she proudly displayed it on her wall which we saw every time we visited. Although Mister Dan didn't mention Mark to many of the residents, he told Miss Janice, and that we wouldn't be back for a while. As we said our goodbyes, Miss Janice also told Mister Dan she'd be praying for him and Mark's family. As we left her room that day, little did we know it would be the last time we would see her. She passed away the next month.

The next day, on Wednesday, we held our R.E.A.D.® session at Rocky Bayou Christian School. At the end of each session Mister Dan told each of our six students that we would not be back for a while, and a substitute R.E.A.D.® Team would be filling in for us. Then Mister Dan told Miss Karen, the Reading Specialist at the school, why we would be gone for a while before we left. She also told Mister Dan that she would keep Mark and his family in her prayers.

We were off on Thursday, but that day I saw the suitcases come out of the downstairs closet. I assumed Mister Dan and Miss Bev were planning a trip, as I heard Miss Bev tell how that was her last day at school. She was taking a leave of absence from teaching for the remainder of the spring semester. I didn't know if I was going along, but as I watched them both pack their suitcases, I sure hoped so.

Early Friday morning Mister Dan loaded Miss Bev's suitcase into the van and left with her. I was concerned, but it wasn't too long before he returned from the airport, alone. He loaded his suitcase into the van, then I got excited when I saw him load my food bin into the back seat floor. He took my leash and harness, looked at me and said, "Road trip, girl!" Oh boy, I was going after all. As it turned out, this would be just the first of four road trips Mister Dan and I would make together from Florida to Colorado and back in 2019.

Two and a half days later we pulled into Mark's driveway in Colorado Springs. As Mister Dan opened the back tailgate of the van and I jumped out, a blast of fresh, cold Colorado air smacked me in the face. Ahh, this is where I belong. I could live here year round! I bounded into the house and there were Maddie and Will running to meet me. They hugged me and loved on me, then Anna, who was not quite walking yet, crawled over to see me. As I lay there, I could see she was not afraid of big dogs, and before long she started to poke me in the face and pull my ears. But I didn't care. I just closed my eyes and took it all in as she proceeded to climb on top of me. I soon discovered a special bond with Anna (my sister). Scott, Mark's older brother, had flown in from his home in the Washington, DC area and was also there. Mister Dan hugged Miss Bev and then gave a big hug to his two sons, especially Mark.

As the family sat and talked that afternoon, I learned that Mark had been diagnosed with liver cancer, as he had a tumor 15 x 17 centimeters that encased almost his entire liver. He had been referred by his local doctor in Colorado Springs to a liver surgeon in Aurora, Colorado, a suburb of Denver, at what's called the Anschutz Cancer Pavilion, part of the University of Colorado Hospital (UC Health), which is the largest hospital in Colorado. He was scheduled to have liver surgery just a few days later, where he would have about two thirds of his liver removed, his spleen, which also showed a tumor, and lymph nodes in the surrounding area. But they were also waiting on results of a biopsy of a lymph node which was taken during a procedure Mark had just had to install a stent in one of his bile ducts, as all were blocked by the tumor, to attempt to relieve his jaundice condition, which it did. That afternoon as I looked out onto Mark's back yard through their sliding glass door, I watched as Mark and Scott threw the football together. Scott had flown all the way from DC just to be there for Mark. I could feel the enduring love that those two brothers had for each other.

The next day, Mark and Jenny got the news that the results of the lymph node biopsy had come back, and the initial diagnosis was wrong! Mark did not have liver cancer but rather Stage Four Non-Hodgkin's Lymphoma, specifically diffuse large B-cell lymphoma (DLBCL), a blood cancer. This was great news, as liver cancer is usually a death sentence. Mark's liver surgery was cancelled, the liver surgeon immediately disappeared from the scene, and a new doctor, a lymphoma oncologist who specializes in blood disorder cancers and is the Clinical Director of Lymphoma Services at Anschutz, Dr. Manali Kamdar, entered the scene. She wanted to meet with Mark and Jenny right away, so they made an appointment to see her in Denver the next day. Dr. Kamdar explained that unlike a solid cancer, for a liquid cancer surgery and even radiation are a waste of time. It can only be treated by chemotherapy or immunotherapy. She wanted to start Mark on a regimen of chemo the very next day, as his PET/CT scan showed that the cancer was not only in his liver and spleen, but had spread to almost the entire right side of his body above the waist. Dr. Kamdar recommended a treatment called R-EPOCH, which stands for the first letter of each drug used in the chemo, way too complicated for this dog to understand. Anyway, this would be a very intense treatment and require six rounds where Mark would be admitted to the hospital for four days each time and then recover at home for the next two weeks before the next round would start. So he would be on a 21-day cycle for the next five months.

Scott had graduated from Niceville High School with a good friend, Daniel Cox. Daniel was a surgeon at the University of Alabama Birmingham (UAB) hospital, and was in charge of the ER there. Scott had kept in touch with Daniel about Mark's condition, and through his contacts, Daniel had arranged a meeting with Mark and Jenny and an oncologist colleague at the MD Anderson Cancer Center in Houston, Texas, considered by many to be the gold standard of cancer treatment centers in the country. Before even meeting with Dr. Kamdar in Denver, Mark had made reservations the next week for he and Jenny to fly to Houston for this appointment. After almost an hour and twenty minutes of their meeting with Dr. Kamdar, Mark told her of their plans to go to Houston for a second opinion. Dr. Kamdar encouraged this, said she would send all the film and reports to whomever they wanted, but also wanted to start Mark on his chemo as soon as they returned. We don't think she ever felt threatened by this plan and believed she would be in charge regardless. But she did tell Mark that if he decided to get treated in Houston, he would have to live there for the next five months. She didn't want him to fly back and forth after each treatment on an airplane to recover at home, as this was too dangerous, with his immune system compromised. As it was, their house in Colorado

Springs was only about an hour and twenty minutes from the hospital in Denver. Plus, if Dr. Kamdar treated him, Mark would have his family to support him at home during each recovery period.

The next night, Jenny came to Mister Dan and told him they had made their decision. They had cancelled their reservations for Houston, felt comfortable with Dr. Kamdar, and were going to stick with her. She said they felt good about their decision, and that there would be no looking back, no second guessing, no what-ifs. Then Mister Dan told me she said something that he will never forget. Jenny looked at Mister Dan that night and said, "And no matter how things turn out, we'll be OK." Mister Dan told me that was the most inspirational definition of faith he had ever heard. He said Jenny and Mark's faith in God and Mister Jesus was strong. He learned that night that real faith does not mean believing that everything will turn out OK. Faith means being OK no matter how things turn out.

For the next eight months Mister Dan and Miss Bev worked out a schedule with Jenny's parents, Mister Dave and Miss Jan, who live outside of Memphis. During that time one set of parents would be with Mark and Jenny, mainly to babysit the kids while Jenny worked at the Mom/Baby Unit at St. Francis Hospital in Colorado Springs as an RN, and Mark recovered at home from his chemo treatments. That's why I got to go to Colorado so often that year. I love Colorado. Mister Dan had to put our therapy dog visits at home mainly on hold, only visiting in between visits to Colorado. We did get to go to school a few times and actually had a little R.E.A.D.® graduation ceremony for my students at Rocky Bayou Elementary. But Mister Dan knew where he needed to be, and so did I.

After only two rounds of R-EPOCH, Mark and Jenny met with Dr. Kamdar. She was ecstatic! Mark's cancer had been reduced by 70%. She was hoping for a 50-60% reduction. The chemo was working. She said that bad things can still happen after the last treatment, but that chance was only about 20%. On July 1st, several weeks after Mark's sixth and last R-EPOCH treatment, he and Jenny met again with Dr. Kamdar, hoping the cancer would be in complete remission. Unfortunately, that was not the case. The bad news was that even though his cancer had been reduced by 90%, the cancer became "smarter" than the chemo he was receiving. Dr. Kamdar explained that the remaining 10% still had to be dealt with, otherwise it could grow and spread and become as bad as it was originally. Traditionally in the past, Mark would have undergone more chemo to prepare his body for an autologous bone marrow transplant (BMT), also called a stem cell transplant, in which the body's own cells are extracted and used in the transplant. In recent years a newer treatment was started called immunotherapy, which could possibly treat Mark's kind of cancer. Dr. Kamdar suggested Mark enter into a clinical trial, which he did. In the trial, there are two randomized groups, and neither Mark nor Dr. Kamdar could choose which group he entered first. The subjects are randomized by computer 50/50 into each of the two groups. The first "Arm,"

"Arm A," is called BMT, and "Arm B" is called CAR (Chimeric Antigen Receptor) T immunotherapy. We were all hoping Mark would be randomized into Arm B, but he wasn't. In order to have the bone marrow transplant, he had to undergo three more rounds of chemo called RICE, which again stands for the chemicals used. RICE is three times stronger than the R-EPOCH that he had just undergone. Like the previous treatments, he would be on a 21-day cycle, with hospitalization in Denver, this time for only three days, followed by two weeks of recovery at home. If, at the end of the three RICE treatments, he was cancer free, only then would he be undergo the BMT. If not, he would be crossed over into Arm B and the CAR-T immunotherapy.

Following the three RICE treatments, on September 19th Mark had his next PET/CT scan and met with Dr. Kamdar. She went straight to the point and let Mark and Jenny know that the cancer was still present, but was now pretty much localized to his liver. This was devastating news. In the past, if you had a stem cell transplant while still showing cancer on a PET scan, your chance of remission following the transplant was less than 15%. But it was the only thing they had to offer. Now there's CAR-T, so Mark was moved to Arm B of the clinical trial.

About a week later, after Mark was approved to cross over into Arm B, he underwent three days of low dose chemo. He was then admitted into the hospital for the CAR-T infusion. Following the infusion, he was required to be within

30 miles of the hospital and have a full-time caregiver with him 24/7, as the side effects of CAR-T can be life-threatening. Jenny asked if Mister Dan could come out and be Mark's caregiver in Denver, as she wanted to remain at home with her kids and continue to work if possible. Of course, Mister Dan agreed. He flew out in early October to be with Mark during his CAR-T infusion and for the next 30 days in Denver, while Mister Dave and Miss Jan came, again, to watch the kids in Colorado Springs. Unfortunately, I didn't get to go with him this time and had to stay home. But I was with Miss Bev, who had gone back to teaching that fall semester at the college, so all was good. I just missed him.

Mister Dan arrived in Denver in time for Mark's CAR-T infusion in the hospital. He told me later that it was quite the procedure. Mark had his blood drawn weeks earlier as soon as he entered the clinical trial. During the blood draw, his T cells were collected by a process called apheresis. T cells are called the "killer cells," because they recognize and kill the cancer cells that all humans have in their bodies. Unfortunately, in Mark's case, the T cells no longer recognized the cancer. His T cells were then sent to a lab, injected with an antigen, and genetically reengineered to make millions more T cells to attack the remaining cancer. This takes about three weeks in the lab, and the blood is then refrigerated and stored until needed. During the CAR-T infusion that day in the hospital, there were six different medical professionals present in Mark's room. The lab technician entered with the container from the Seattle lab that had stored the two vials that would be infused into Mark's port. As he took each vial out and thawed it, he explained that the infusion had to be completed within two hours, or the cells would "expire." He handed the first vial to the nurse, and everyone held their breath as she transferred the clear liquid from the vial into a syringe she would use for the injection. She then took exactly four minutes and thirty seconds to inject Mark with this liquid gold. The same procedure was used for a second vial. These two vials, Mister Dan was told, were worth nearly half a million dollars! Following the infusion, Mark was closely monitored in the hospital for the next 24 hours for any side effects.

Mister Dan had previously arranged to stay with Mark on Buckley AFB at a Temporary Lodging Facility (TLF) called The Rocky Mountain Lodge, as he is retired Air Force and has that privilege. Buckley is only about 5 miles from the hospital, so it was a perfect setup with a suite of two bedrooms, bathroom, living room, dining room, and full kitchen. The next day Mister Dan got a call from Mark that he was ready to be released from the hospital. They stayed at the Buckley TLF for the next 30 days, and amazingly, Mark had absolutely no side effects from the CAR-T. In fact, Jenny and the kids came up for a sleep-over on two of the weekends they were up there. Mark is a great cook, so they had good meals together, and Mister Dan took Mark to the Buckley gym and they worked out together every day that the gym was open for about an hour and a half each day. It was only closed for a couple days about half way through their stay due to a snow storm that hit the Denver area. Mister Dan figured eating right and exercise were crucial to Mark's recovery.

After the 30 days were up, Mister Dan drove Mark home to Colorado Springs and flew home to Florida the next day. I was ecstatic when he walked through the door. We would get back to our normal routine and continue our therapy dog visits each week. Mark and Jenny got back into their normal routine after Mister Dave and Miss Jan left the day after Mister Dan left. After months of hospitalizations, chemo, and CAR-T, Mark finally went back to work. He looked great, as his hair had grown back and he even started a cool beard, which he had to immediately shave when he continued his duty as an Air Force Reserve Major at Schriever AFB in Colorado Springs. He still couldn't drive for another 30 days (60 days from his CAR-T infusion) due to side effects, which could include seizures, up to that time. But he had a friend who lived in his neighborhood who drove him to work, as they both worked in the Contracting Office at the Air Force Academy. By early December Mark was back to driving himself again. The next major milestone would occur early in the new year. On December 30th Mark had his next PET/CT scan and on January 2nd, 2020, almost a year after this nightmare had begun, he and Jenny went to Denver to meet again with Dr. Kamdar to find out the results.

At this point, I'd like to turn the narration over to Mister Dan for the next few paragraphs of this chapter, as he has some things he'd like to share that would better come from him than from me. As a dog, sometimes you just have to defer to your human partner when sharing human emotions. So Mister Dan, over to you.

Thanks, Elsa. We published Elsa's original book in January of 2020 before we were able to finish this chapter with hopes and prayers that this nightmare would all end well. In the next few paragraphs I will conclude this chapter of our lives and these next few pages are the reason we've published a "Revised Edition" to Elsa's book. So here goes.

I wish I could say this chapter has a happy ending, but it doesn't. Jenny and Mark found out from Dr. Kamdar on January 2nd that the CAR-T immunotherapy had failed with the cancer remaining in his liver and two new spots that had grown as well. It was not present anywhere else, but the fact that there were two new spots indicated that the cancer was "smarter" than the treatment. Dr. Kamdar laid out further treatment options and Mark and Jenny considered those. Then a few weeks later another clinical trial became available which was also a CAR-T immunotherapy treatment. This would normally not be available to a patient who had already gone through CAR-T, but since Mark's first CAR-T used his own T cells and this trial used a donor's cells, he qualified. He underwent a second CAR-T immunotherapy treatment but after about a month, discovered this treatment, too, had failed to produce the hoped-for results of complete remission. At this point, there was nothing more the doctors could do.

The third week of March Bev and I flew out to Colorado Springs to be with Mark and his family during Bev's Spring Break from the college. While there the corona pandemic raised its ugly head and Bev's college extended their Spring Break and began on-line classes only. They would eventually shut down all face-to-face classes through the end of the semester. Since we didn't have to get back to Niceville for Bev to teach (she was doing everything on-line) we stayed a few extra days. But the day we did fly back to Florida, Mark's temperature spiked to 104 degrees and he was taken by ambulance to the hospital when his blood pressure dropped to 40/20. He had contracted Cdiff, a deadly virus, as well as pneumonia. Because of Covid 19 patients already admitted to the hospital, no one was allowed to visit Mark, not even Jenny. We flew back out to the Springs two days later and ended up staying another four weeks. Mark was in the hospital for ten days, and when he was released he had recovered from his pneumonia and the Cdiff infection, but he was extremely weak. In the almost 16 months since this nightmare started, I had never seen Mark look so bad. He improved slowly, was able to eat solid food again, and finally was well enough to be up and about and enjoy some time with his family. Scott flew out from his home in DC and spent about a week with his little brother. They reminisced for hours about their childhood, growing-up years, college years and beyond. During these precious moments with Mark telling some hilarious stories, Scott recorded their conversations on audio tape for Jenny and the kids. After our spending about a month with them, Jenny and Mark wanted some alone time for themselves and their family, so we flew back to Florida. This whole time Elsa stayed home but was well taken care of by two dog sitters who switched off coming to the house to feed her, walk her, and love on her.

Several days after arriving home Jenny called to say that Mark wanted to come home to Florida to spend some time on the beaches that he had grown up near and loved one last time. He had already been enrolled in Hospice home care. We welcomed Jenny and Mark and the three kids about a week later, and Scott and his family had driven down from their home outside of DC as well. Mark's Hospice care was transferred from Colorado Springs to Niceville. The plan was for our family to be with them for the first week and then for Jenny's family to come and spend the second week with them in a condo they would rent on the beach before Mark and his family flew back to Colorado. We had a wonderful time that first week, and one of Mark's closest friends from high school had driven down from his home in Columbus, Ohio to spend some time with Mark as well. We celebrated several days on the beach that first week. But after Scott and his family left, Mark's condition worsened and he was too weak to go to the condo or the beach after Jenny's family arrived. So the kids went out to the condo with Jenny's parents and two brothers and their cousins, while Jenny stayed at our home with Mark. The kids would come to visit Mark every day. It quickly became obvious he was also too weak to fly home.

Two days after they arrived home, Scott made reservations to fly back to Florida to be with his brother. Bev and I took turns with Jenny throughout the next couple of days and nights being with Mark 24/7, as he was now too weak to get up or walk on his own. Scott arrived back on a Monday afternoon, and that evening and all night long we all spent with Mark. A hospital bed had been set up for Mark in the TV room downstairs. Normally, Elsa goes upstairs to sleep in our bedroom with us, or in the toilet room off the master bath, as she's mentioned earlier, after I go upstairs to bed. But this night, she stayed downstairs and lay right beside Mark's bed while each of us, in turn, lay with and petted her to gain the strength and comfort she provided. Elsa knew.

It was 3:41 AM on Tuesday, May 12, 2020. I was there. Bev was there. Scott was there. His children were with him in his heart. And Jenny lay beside him as Mark took his last breath. She put her head on his chest to listen for a heartbeat, and said, "He's gone."

Mark's smile could light up an entire room! His gentle, quiet demeanor was paired perfectly with his sense of humor. Mark enjoyed the outdoors, biking, skiing, watching football, and enjoying friends and family. He worked hard and his leadership skills were one of his biggest strengths. He was currently working at the US Air Force Academy as a Contracting Specialist and as a Major in the Air Force Reserves. Mark took great pride in being a family man and loved being involved in everything his children did. He is and will always be his children's hero.

Above all, Mark was a Christian, as is Jenny. Mark accepted Jesus into his life in the sixth grade at a church Youth Group retreat called Meltdown at the Laguna Beach Retreat Center in Panama City Beach, FL. I know because I was there that night. You see, rather than just drop my sons off at church Youth Group every Wednesday night and pick them up afterwards, I wanted to be involved with them. So for ten years I was a Youth Counselor for our Youth Group at what was then Niceville United Methodist Church, now Crosspoint, the whole time Mark and his older brother Scott were coming up through the ranks of middle and high school. I always believed the greatest gift any parent could give his child is the gift of Jesus Christ. So my wife Bev and I tried to model Jesus in our lives for our boys in hopes that one day, they would accept Jesus for themselves into their hearts. I'm eternally grateful that both my sons did. Jenny is doing the same thing for her and Mark's children, Maddie, now age 8, William, age 6, and Anna, only 2. Mark was the most courageous person I've ever known, and he fought every day to the very end. He NEVER gave up! But make no mistake – CANCER DID NOT WIN. DEATH DID NOT WIN. THE RESURRECTION OF JESUS CHRIST HAS WON, and Mark is with his Jesus now. And one day, I will be reunited with my son.

As I write this, I can honestly say I'm not mad at God. I never have been. This wasn't his FAULT. In fact, for the first time in my life, I understand how God felt when he watched His son suffer and die on the Cross, just as I watched as my son suffered and died in his bed. God has felt my pain, and He loved Mark just as much as He loved His own son. If I'm angry with anyone it's we humans who have polluted, decimated, and otherwise destroyed the perfect planet that God gave us, including His animals, and have created the epidemic that cancer has become in this country, more so than any other country in the world, just in the past 70 years of my lifetime.

Ever since this ordeal started, we've had prayers pouring in from all over the country from Mark and Jenny's family and friends to our family and friends. I've already tried on Facebook to thank all of you. But above all, thank you to Scott. Although you two fought like a couple of tom cats growing up, Mark idolized you, and he couldn't have asked for a better big brother. I especially saw Mark's love for you when he entered the 9th grade and you left for Wake. You'd call home from college and talk to Mom and me for a few minutes, then we'd hand the phone off to Mark, he'd go into his bedroom, and talk to you for the longest time. He missed you so much. You cast a large shadow for him in high school after winning two state championships in weightlifting and setting the school pole vault record. But I know you were Mark's biggest fan when he broke your pole vault school record and won his own state title his junior year. After that track meet at Florida Field in Gainesville, you were the first one he called to share his joy. I missed many of your college track meets because I was attending Mark's high school meets held at the same time. He followed in your footsteps and finally won the Most Outstanding Male Athlete Award upon graduation from Niceville High School in 2001, the same award you had won four years earlier. He modeled his collegiate athletic career after yours. Even though many miles separated you after high school, you kept in close touch, and you have been there for Mark every day during his fight for his life. But above all, the most precious gift you ever gave to Mark and his family were those audio tapes that you recorded during your special moments with him in his last days. These will be a priceless gift for Maddie, Will, and Anna ten years from now as they listen over and over to remember their Daddy and begin to understand who he was and how much he loved them. Indeed, Mark was one of a kind and one who will never be forgotten!

Finally, before I turn it back over to Elsa, I'd like to announce that all the proceeds and royalties that I receive from Elsa's book, and from my first book, *IT TOOK A DOG*, by Dan Holmes, available on Amazon, will go to Jenny and the kids. So thank you for purchasing this book. If you have occasion to tell any of your family or friends about this book, or my previous book, even if they don't read them, just ordering them on Amazon will be money well spent.

That's all I wanted to say, so I'll turn it back over to you, Elsa, to complete this and The Last Chapter.

Thanks Mister Dan. I know how hard that was for you to write. I'll finish up now.

Several years ago a brilliant human by the name of W. Bruce Cameron wrote a great dog book called *A DOG'S PURPOSE*. It's subtitle is *Every dog happens for a reason.* This book was so popular it hit the New York Times' Best Seller List and was made into a Hollywood movie. In the book, and the movie, a little abandoned puppy is picked up by a thoughtless human who puts it into the back seat of his pickup truck. He proceeds to park and go into a bar to drink with his friends, leaving the dog in the truck with the windows rolled up. It's a stifling hot day, the truck cab heats up, and the little dog is about to suffocate, his tongue hanging out. A female human happens along, sees what is happening, smashes the back window of the truck and rescues the little dog. She takes him home and convinces her husband to let their young son Ethan keep the dog. Ethan and Bailey grow up together, become best friends, and do everything together. Finally, Ethan is grown and goes off to college. While there, Bailey crosses the rainbow bridge. But that's not the end of the story. The dog is reincarnated and comes back as a different dog, born into a different family with different responsibilities. This happens two or three more times, and each time the dog has to discover its own purpose. But in the end, I think the message is clear – every dog's purpose is basically the same.

Mister Dan has called me a hero to thousands of humans across Northwest Florida, from the older humans at The Manor to the little humans at the Children's Advocacy Center; from my R.E.A.D.® students at school to the strangers I meet every week at the airport and will probably never see again. I don't know if all that's true, but I do know this. I believe God put me on this earth and brought me into Mister Dan's life, and into the lives of his family, for just such a time as this. Indeed, I have found my purpose.

Our R.E.A.D. Graduation at Rocky Bayou Christian School

R.E.A.D.ing my Favorite Book

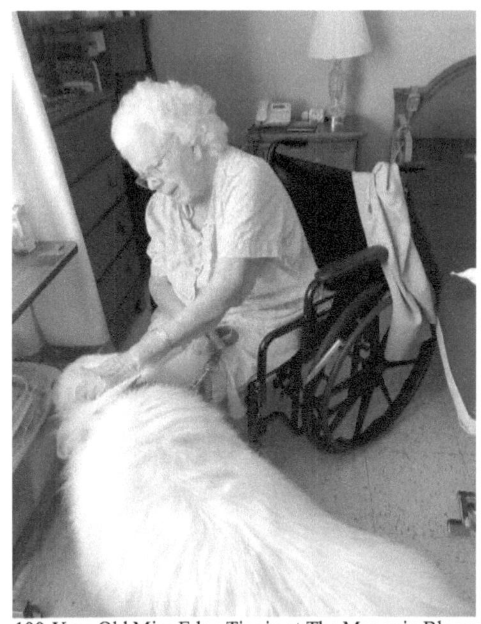
Visiting 100-Year-Old Miss Edna Tippin at The Manor in Bluewater Bay

Mister Dan and Me at the Okaloosa County Courthouse

Anna, Mark's Daughter, and Me in Colorado Springs

Maddie, Will, Anna and Me at Their House in Colorado Springs

I LOVE Colorado!!

Anna, Will, Maddie, Miss Bev, Mister Dan and Me

Mark and His Family, December 2019

Mark Holmes, December 21, 1982 – May 12, 2020

The Last Chapter

I could tell story after story of some of the over 300 therapy dog team visits I have been on with Mister Dan. He told me this story after he and Miss Bev got home from a trip, and I didn't think I even had much to do with it. But I'll let you be the judge.

It was the week before Christmas 2018 and Mister Dan and Miss Bev were going to visit their oldest son Scott, his wife Lauren, and their two grandkids at their home up in the Washington D.C. suburb of Aldie, Virginia. They had just been up there with me visiting a couple months before and had met Wyatt, their new grandson who had just been born about a month earlier. But Lauren had taken off work from mid-September when he was born until after Thanksgiving to care for him before going back to work, and Scott took off work the first two weeks of December to care for him so they wouldn't have to start him in daycare before the first of the new year. So neither of them had any vacation time left. Knowing they couldn't go anywhere over the holidays, Mister Dan and Miss Bev decided to visit them. They were only going to be gone for a week (they flew up on a Saturday and flew home the next Saturday), so I didn't get to go. They left me home with dog sitters. After only three days, my normal dog sitter Miss Gina, who I love, was going to Disney World with her family, so Mister Dan arranged for our neighbor next door, Kelsey, a beautiful girl who was home on Christmas break with her parents from Florida State University, to watch me. Kelsey and I had a great time too.

About half way through their trip, on Wednesday, Mister Dan got a call from Miss Angela, the Activities Director at The Manor. She asked if he was in town. He told her no, he was up in Virginia visiting family, and asked what was up. She said, "That's too bad." Apparently an elderly woman, a German lady whom we visited with each week at The Manor, had fallen gravely ill. She was taken to Twin Cities Hospital in Niceville and was placed into Hospice care. She only had a few days left to live. Although her best friend was with her, she was asking to see me, Elsa, the dog! I was shocked when Mister Dan told me this after he got home. He told Miss Angela he was so sorry, but he'd check back in with her at the end of the week. On Friday he called back and Miss Angela told him she was still hanging on. Mister Dan promised to call the hospital the next day when he got home.

The next day both of Mister Dan and Miss Bev's flights were delayed, so when they finally walked through the front door at home, it was almost midnight. They were both exhausted. I ran to greet them and was so excited to see them, but they didn't want to play. They both just wanted to go to bed. The next morning, as soon as he got up, Mister Dan called the hospital at 7:00 AM. When the Charge Nurse answered and heard the name Elsa, she immediately knew who I was. She told Mister Dan that unfortunately, the lady had passed away at 2:00 AM that morning.

Mister Dan was so sad that he didn't get home in time to take me to see this lady. But he looked at me that Sunday morning and said, "See, girl, what an impact you're having on people's lives?" Here was this lady, who I'm embarrassed to say I hardly remember, as there are many other residents at The Manor with whom I have an even closer bond, literally on her deathbed and asking to see me, Elsa, the therapy dog! I was humbled. But like Mister Dan, I was also sad. Not sad that I missed seeing her, but more sad to think that I was the one she wanted to see in her last hours. Wasn't there another human who she wanted to see more? Wasn't there someone else more important in her life? I guess the unconditional love humans feel when they pet me must be special, and like Mister Dan said, I guess I have become a big part of many lives. Sad as it is, I fear some humans who I've met will remember me as much as anyone else they have in their lives.

In his first book *IT TOOK A DOG*, by Dan Holmes, available on Amazon, Mister Dan gave me the ultimate compliment when he said, "I don't want this to sound trite or trivial, but when I see Elsa, I see Jesus." Mister Dan told me that Mister Jesus is really God, but he came to earth as a human to show other humans what God is like. When I approach a stranger, like at the airport (where there are *lots* of strangers), I don't see the color of his skin. I can't. Like all dogs, I'm colorblind! Maybe that's why God made us that way. If she's wearing a head scarf, that means nothing to me. All I care about is being petted. And if that human pets me, I'll be his friend for life. I guess that's the way it is with Mister Jesus. If you just trust Him and ask Him into your life, He'll be a friend that will never leave you. So, I guess like Mister Jesus, the unconditional love I have for humans just comes naturally.

Love. Now that's a subject I could talk about all day. Again, in his first book *IT TOOK A DOG*, by Dan Holmes, available on Amazon, Mister Dan said this: "I love Elsa, and I tell her so often. Especially at night, before I crawl into bed, I'll find Elsa wherever she is on the floor, usually in our bedroom or walk-in closet. I'll bend down, hold her head in my hands and kiss her face while telling her over and over that I love her. I want her to know and understand those words. And I think she loves me."

What? Wait a minute. Hold the presses. What did you say? I think she loves me. *I think she loves me.* Mister Dan, do you have $#*! for brains? Of course I love you! I'd give my very *life* for you. If we were out alone together, especially at night, and someone physically attacked you, unless he had a knife or a gun, he'd be dead meat! I'd rip his throat out. Why do you think I follow you all over the house just to be close to you? Why do I sleep next to your bed at night? Why do I even like to have eye contact with you while you're in the shower (calm down ladies, it's no big deal, TRUST ME!)? I love you more than life itself. And let this be a lesson for all dog owners. If you love your dog, feed it, water it, and give it safe shelter, rest assured your dog loves you. And you can take that to the bank! I will love you, Mister Dan, until my dying day, and beyond.

So that begs the age-old question – are there dogs in heaven? Well, a wise and very funny human, Will Rogers, once said, "If there are no dogs in heaven, then when I die, I want to go where they are." Of course there are dogs in heaven. And you can take that to the bank too! I look forward to meeting all of Mister Dan's previous dogs when I cross the rainbow bridge, including Mittens, Scarlett, Lucky, Tux, and Kinky. And I know I'll be reunited with Mark and Mister Dan someday. Now we dogs don't live as long as you humans would like us to. I think that's because humans are born so they can learn how to live a good life – like being nice and loving unconditionally. Well, we dogs already know how to do that, so we don't have to stay around for as long as you do.

When I was out in Colorado last summer with Mister Dan at Mark's house for about six weeks helping him babysit his three grandkids, I loved the Colorado summers – they were much cooler than they are here in Florida. He'd take me for a walk every morning and every afternoon, just like he does here at home. On one of our afternoon walks we were passing a house with a UPS truck out front. The driver came back to his truck after delivering a package, we said hi, and he told Mister Dan to wait a minute. He went into his truck and came back out with a treat for me. I was thrilled! Then a few days later, we saw this same truck in the neighborhood and he stopped, without even a package to deliver, got out and gave me a treat again. I was beyond thrilled! About a week after that I was relaxing on the front porch with Mark and Mister Dan, and this same truck actually stopped at the house to deliver a package to Mark and Jenny. I ran to the truck and the wonderful driver greeted me, by name, with a hug and went back into his truck to get me another treat. I loved this guy. Fast forward about two months. Mister Dan had gone back to Colorado to be with Mark near the hospital in Denver for 30 days. I didn't get to go this time and stayed home with Miss Bev, who had gone back to teaching at the college. She also walked me every morning and afternoon when she got home from work. Low and behold, on one of our afternoon walks I saw this *same* UPS truck delivering packages in our very own neighborhood! I tried to escape to the truck and get my treat from the wonderful driver but Miss Bev held tight to my leash laughing all the while. I remembered what Brown had done for me. What can Brown do for you?

As I've said before, I don't remember much about my past. But I do remember a dream I had recently. And yes, dogs do dream. Any dog owner knows this. Just watch a dog when it sleeps. She'll twitch and shake, and sometimes even wake up barking. You can bet when it does that she's finally caught the squirrel she's been chasing for months before it got to the tree. Now that she's got it in her mouth, she's just trying to figure out what to do with it. But I digress, as I've been known to do. This dream started out really great. Soon after my book was published, sales were brisk. In fact, it didn't take long for the sales of my book to surpass those of Mister Dan's first book *IT TOOK A DOG*, by Dan Holmes, *still* available on Amazon. That's probably because Mister Dan bought close to two hundred copies of his book just to give away to family and friends. Anyway, in my dream, Kelsey, the girl next door who dog sat for me and was now a senior at FSU, read my book and liked it. She posted it on her Facebook page, and it went viral all over the FSU campus. Then it spread to college campuses all across Florida, then Alabama and Georgia, and all across the southeast. Before you know it, my book had hit the New York Times' Best Seller List! Then Scott, Mister Dan's oldest son who had spent five years in Hollywood after he graduated from Wake Forest dabbling in acting and screenwriting, wrote a screen play based on my book. He sent it to an actor friend, and Carter in turn gave it to a Hollywood producer. The producer liked it and hired a director. I was going to be a movie star, and become a very rich pooch. And I was going to take care of Jenny and her kids for the rest of their lives from the residuals. But then the director came to me and broke the news that he had hired another dog, a younger Great Pyrenees, to play my part. I woke up convulsing and growling, demanding all the while that I play myself!

So we come to the end of my story. That's a wrap, in Hollywood speak. I've said what I wanted to say, so it's time to get off the stage. I hope you've enjoyed what you've read. But more importantly, I hope you've learned something. I hope you've learned something about the canine species and especially about the Great Pyrenees, the best dogs....ever! I think we dogs have a lot to teach you humans. But more importantly, I hope you've learned something about yourself. I know I've learned a lot in writing my book. In fact, I've found the answer some of the most important questions I've ever had in my life. How did I go from a hopelessly lost, malnourished, diseased and stinky stray to the beautiful white Great Pyrenees I am today? How was I given a second chance at life? How was I cured of my heartworm? How did I lose my matted, tangled, filthy fur so I could grow a beautiful new coat? How did I become a well-trained, well-mannered therapy dog? How have I found a peace, contentment, and pure joy in my life? Why does every day feel like a new adventure that I just can't wait to experience? But maybe most important of all, how did I find my forever home where I feel safe and loved?

It took a human.

ABOUT THE AUTHOR

Elsa Holmes is living large in Niceville, Florida with her forever family Mister Dan and Miss Bev Holmes. Elsa has her own email account and she would love to hear from you. If you write to her, she promises to write back. She can be reached at elsadog@cox.net.